Fully Alive

Other books by or about John Main from Canterbury Press

Monastery Without Walls: The Spiritual Letters of John Main
Edited by Laurence Freeman OSB
Complete and unabridged edition

Door to Silence: An Anthology for Christian Meditation
Edited and introduced by Laurence Freeman OSB
A new collection of quotations from the writings of John Main

Word into Silence: A Manual for Christian Meditation
Edited by Laurence Freeman OSB
A spiritual classic on the art of contemplation

John Main: The Expanding Vision
Edited by Laurence Freeman OSB and Stefan Reynolds
Celebrating a remarkable legacy of spiritual teaching

The Heart of Creation: Meditation: A Way of Setting God Free in the World
Edited by Laurence Freeman

Word Made Flesh: Recovering a Sense of the Sacred through Prayer
Introduction by Laurence Freeman

Moment of Christ: Prayer as the Way to God's Fullness
Edited by Laurence Freeman

The Way of Unknowing: Expanding the Spiritual Horizons Through Meditation
Introduction by Laurence Freeman

www.canterburypress.co.uk

Fully Alive

John Main

Edited by
Laurence Freeman

CANTERBURY
PRESS
Norwich

© John Main 2013

First published in 2013 by the Canterbury Press Norwich
Editorial office
3rd Floor, Invicta House,
108–114 Golden Lane,
London EC1Y 0TG

Canterbury Press is an imprint of Hymns Ancient & Modern Ltd
(a registered charity)
13A Hellesdon Park Road, Norwich,
Norfolk NR6 5DR, UK

www.canterburypress.co.uk

British Library Cataloguing in Publication data

A catalogue record for this book is available
from the British Library

978 1 84825 559 3

Typeset by Manila Typesetting
Printed and bound in Great Britain by
CPI Group (UK) Ltd, Croydon

Contents

Introduction   vii

Part 1 In the Beginning

  1 The Sound of the Mantra   3
  2 Still a Beginner   7
  3 The Way of Enlightenment   10
  4 Total Potential   13
  5 Experience and Expansion   16
  6 Purity of Heart   20
  7 Our Two Lives   23
  8 Heart-Longing   26
  9 Wholly Present   30
 10 Questions   34
 11 The School of Cassian   39
 12 The Delicate Balance   44

Part 2 Being on the Way

 13 Life as Revelation   51
 14 Questions   55
 15 The Prodigal Son   60
 16 The Idea of Progress   62
 17 The Secure Base   65
 18 Attention   68

19 Shiva's Tale of Salvation   71
20 Being a Pilgrim   74

Part 3 Fully Alive
21 Beginning for the First Time Again   79
22 Fullness of Life   83
23 Seeking Truth   86
24 Dispossession   89

Bibliography   91
Books and CDs by or about John Main   93
About the World Community for
Christian Meditation   95
The World Community for Christian Meditation 97

Introduction

In editing these talks, which were originally given to weekly meditation groups meeting at his monastery, I have once again been moved and inspired by the depth and richness of John Main's simplicity. I think many people around the world who already see John Main as an important guide in their own spiritual journey will feel encouraged and strengthened, by his clarity and conviction, to commit themselves further to the inner journey they have begun.

I hope, too, that on their contemplative pilgrimage many more will meet him as a teacher through these words which are directed not to more words and thoughts but to entering the work of silence in regular times of practice.

John Main is an interesting teacher for our time. He is deeply traditional and his Christian faith very personal, heartfelt and explicit. He bewails the way many Christians underestimate the mystery and wonder of their faith. In a post-Christendom culture where Christianity is not cool and often embarrassing this is challenging. Yet he juxtaposes unexpected elements alongside this declaration of faith: an emphasis on experience, a demanding yet realistic call to see meditation as a spiritual discipline (twice a day) and asceticism for the twenty-first century.

John Main in these teachings was concerned to encourage people to start and to restart their practice. Like his fourth-century master, John Cassian, he believed that 'experience is the teacher'. Yet his reinforcement of this experiential approach is often punctuated by startling paradoxes. 'What does fullness need in order to develop? Emptiness.'

Experience for him did not mean temporarily altered states of consciousness during meditation but a process of radical transformation of life. No less than modern scientists researching the effects of meditation on the brain and behaviour, he was convinced that meditation changes us for the better. He goes much further than scientists, however, by seeing the potential for transformation as infinite. For him meditation doesn't only make you feel better it reveals the meaning of goodness and the ultimate meaning of love.

He is a humanist yet he sees that the fullness of humanity launches us into the mystery of being itself. Christ – in whom and through whom we can enter this mystery – is for him both an intimate and cosmic presence. John Main was well aware that he might seem to be making great claims for this simple daily practice. But he was authentic, he spoke from experience and he knew it was an experience open to all.

I will never forget the first time he spoke to me about meditation. I was at university and on a largely intellectual search for truth and meaning. When he described meditation I could sense the horizons of my understanding shifting. Intellectually I could make no sense of it at all. It even seemed nonsensical, though that was also fascinating because of what my heart was telling me. It told me this was real and genuine and I longed to know it in my own experience.

I hope that many readers of this book will be similarly disturbed and enriched by what he says and the deceptively simple way in which he says it.

Laurence Freeman OSB

PART I

In the Beginning

I

The Sound of the Mantra

One of the astonishing things about meditation is that it is so extraordinarily simple to understand. And yet it appears difficult for many people to appreciate the utter simplicity of it.

We recommend that you come to one of our introductory groups for about twelve weeks to learn about the basic way of meditation. But at the end of that time each of us is still a beginner. So, it is just as important twelve weeks, or indeed twelve years, later to be clear about the sheer simplicity of the way. It is also necessary to be very humble about the way: to accept it and not try to change it around or water it down to suit you.

This is the way of meditation: take your mantra, your word, and recite it continuously. However peaceful you may be feeling, recite it. However drowsy you are feeling, recite it. However difficult it is to say, recite it. However much you are getting out of it, or however little you are getting out of it, recite your word. If you can understand that, you will understand almost all there is to understand of the basic doctrine: to say your mantra from beginning to end. You must also meditate every morning and every evening. If you seriously want to set out on the path that the tradition puts before us, then you need to make that time available every morning and every evening. Everything beyond that is more or less obvious. You must also learn to sit absolutely still in order to enter into the experience of a total stillness of body and spirit, of the whole person.

Meditation is our way of total entry into the present moment. All of us tend to live in the past or in the future. Live neither in the past nor in the future. Learn to be present wholly to the present moment, to the now, to the now that we can describe as the eternal now of God. Unhappiness comes generally from our refusal to be in the now. Even suffering has its meaning and unless we accept it fully, in its moment, we will have had the experience but missed the meaning. This is why we have to learn to listen to the mantra with total attention. It is a narrowing down of our consciousness to a single point: the pointedness of the single sound of the mantra. That is what we learn to do by saying the mantra.

Maranatha: ma-ra-na-tha

Listen to it with total and deepening attention and in a growing simplicity and humility. The mantra is like one drop of water in a mighty river and like that single drop it contains the whole river within itself: right back to the source and to the ocean. The faithfully repeated mantra, like the drops of water in a mighty river, is always new and yet always the same.

To take the example a step further, the river is the river of life that flows out from the Father and returns to this source. By being wholly present to ourselves and fully conscious in the moment, the mystery unfolds. As we say our mantra we are fully open to eternal reality. Even more than that – and this is the great vision proclaimed by Jesus – we *enter into* that ever-present reality. In his teaching Jesus is clear that there is a spring of water welling up in our hearts to eternal life and if we can learn to drink from that water we shall never thirst.

> He that believes in me, as the scripture has said, out of his heart shall flow rivers of living water. (John 7.38)

In the power given to us from that spring we have everything we need to develop all the talents we have been given and so to lead our lives to the full. Meditation is simply being open to that spring of living water in your own heart. As I say, we have to learn to be humble. Learning just to say the word is a great training in humility.

In meditation we give up making wonderful speeches to God. We give up all our ratiocination about the nature of God and we are content, like a child, to say one little word; the word I recommend is *maranatha* (pronounced in four equal syllables *ma-ra-na-tha*). It is learning this humility that teaches us not to be daunted by the scale of the work. We are a group of very ordinary people yet we are talking about the eternal reality of God present in our own hearts. We need to learn not to be intoxicated by the wonder of the vision but to tread the path on a daily basis by returning each morning and evening to the sheer ordinariness of saying our word.

What I would say to you, therefore, as we begin is: learn to say your mantra with growing simplicity and humility. Learn to be content with the simplicity and the poverty of the one little word. Everything else, you let go of. Letting go of all your past and of all your plans for the future you enter into the present moment, the moment where the *now* of God's infinite love is flowing in your mind and heart with a power greater than that of the mightiest river or waterfall in the world. All we have to learn is to enter in. The power of that great river of love, of that water welling up to eternal life, will sweep us beyond ourselves. We know not where.

But what we do know is that by wholly opening ourselves to its power we will be swept into the mystery of God's infinite love.

Listen to St Paul writing to the Ephesians:

Praise be to the God and Father of our Lord Jesus Christ who has bestowed on us, in Christ, every spiritual blessing in the heavenly realms. In Christ He chose us before the world was founded to be dedicated, to be without blemish in His sight and to be full of love and He destined us, as such was his will and pleasure, to be accepted as His children through Jesus Christ, that the glory of His gracious gift so graciously bestowed on us in His beloved, might resound to His praise. (Eph. 1.3–6)

This is the gift that waits to be found in our hearts. It is the gift of Christ's infinite love. Nothing is more important in our lives – and we learn it by a simple daily discipline – to be open to that love and to receive it with generosity.

2

Still a Beginner

This is St Paul writing to the Romans:

> I discover this principle then: that when I want to do the right only the wrong is within my reach. In my inmost self I delight in the Lord God but I perceive that there is in my bodily members a different law fighting against the law that my reason approves and making me a prisoner under the law. (Rom. 7.21–23)

I want to consider meditation as the way to harmony, the way to transcend the divisions that we encounter within ourselves. To meditate is simplicity itself. When we meditate all we have to do is to say our word, our mantra. First, when you prepare to meditate, sit as comfortably as you can, close your eyes gently and begin to say your word. The word I recommend you to say is *maranatha*. Do not think about anything; do not try to imagine anything. Do not attend to anything at all except the sound of the mantra.

The mantra is just like a harmonic that sounds on the frequency of God and brings us into harmony with the one who is one. However, we all experience divisions within ourselves. One of the most painful things to discover is that we are divided against ourselves. Like St Paul, we experience a divided consciousness. Apart from that there are the divisions imposed on us by our human state: even the division between body and spirit, male and female, black and white, old and young, and so on. It is the clear teaching of the early Christian community that this dividedness within *and* between ourselves is no longer necessary. It is no longer an essential part of the human consciousness. The powerful message of the New Testament is that it is no longer necessary to look at reality through cracked spectacles. There exists a principle of unity.

There is a way to cross every chasm that divides us. So often we think that if we are divided we have to opt for one of the polarities of our divided state. Will we opt for the right thing or the wrong thing, for love or for hate, for concern or indifference? But what the New Testament says to us is that there is another option – one open to every one of us. It involves going deeper within ourselves, beyond the surface dividedness. What each of us is called to is to learn to live out of this deeper unity of our human spirit.

It involves even more than that. It involves learning to live out of the wholly undivided consciousness of Christ; and to live from our own experience the truth of what Christ meant when he said, 'The Father and I are one' (John 10.30).

This is what Christian meditation is about: learning to meet reality from the integral harmony of Christ. The result for us is astonishing because all the divisions – body, spirit, male, female, black, white, old, young – all of these divisions are resolved in a person and through the power of the presence within us of the person of Jesus Christ.

Meditation is learning to be sensitive to and aware of his presence within us. It is this presence that teaches us that each of us is made a real person by the power of his love. If we can make contact with those depths within us we discover that we are not just autonomous, isolated persons. Each of us, in this mystery of Christ dwelling in our hearts, is called to love and to be loved beyond all division.

So, why meditation? The key to all this is the essential principle of harmony to be found within us. That principle is the Spirit, the spirit of Christ. Meditation is simply the way of focusing, not just our attention, but our lives too, on that principle of harmony, unity and love.

In order to take the journey seriously it is essential to meditate every morning and every evening. There are no short cuts. There is no instant mysticism; but there is the reality of the pilgrimage to your own heart. In meditation you are not asked to accept someone else's experience second-hand, not even the testimony of the apostles or of St Paul. Each of us is invited to plumb these depths, to make contact with the Spirit of Christ ourselves, in our own experience. In that process we become wholly real, wholly the person we are called to be. In that process of living out of the power of Christ all division is transcended.

Listen to St Paul again:

The conclusion of the matter is this: there is no condemnation for those who are united with Christ Jesus, because in Christ Jesus the life-giving law of the Spirit has set you free from the law of sin and death. What the law could never do . . . God has done: by sending his own Son in a form like that of our own sinful nature, and as a sacrifice for sin. (Rom. 8.1–3)

We undertake this journey in faith. We travel in faith. We arrive in faith. Our faith is in the Spirit who dwells in our hearts and who in silence is loving to all.

Remember the way: from the beginning to the end of each meditation, each morning and evening, say your mantra, say your word, *maranatha*. Do not think, do not imagine. But be. Be in the presence and be in the power of the presence.

3

The Way of Enlightenment

Let us reflect about meditation as the way of enlightenment. That might sound like an extraordinary statement. But if you look at the Gospels and the New Testament in general, they do propose an extraordinary thesis. It is that the ordinary destiny of every man and woman alive is to be filled with the light of Christ and to learn to see everything by that light.

The New Testament proposes that this is the task of every Christian life: to learn to see ourselves, to see others, to see everything by the power of this life which is Christ. The New Testament proposes that this light of Christ is a very powerful light that burns away darkness and dispels all shadows. The peculiar power of the light of Christ is that it reveals to us reality as it is. Light is a form of energy that makes vision possible; the brighter the light the clearer the vision, the deeper the harmony. What we learn is that Christ is our light. The task of Christian meditation is simply to uncover the brilliance of the light of Christ in our own hearts.

But we must understand this carefully. Everything that God gives us is pure gift. The gift of our own being. The gift to know of his existence. And the incredible gift that we have been given: of knowing that he is love. The task of Christian life is to be as fully open as possible to all these good gifts. So, we come to our times of meditation not looking for experiences, even the experience of light or enlightenment. We come to meditation to understand how each of us makes contact with what is essential in our lives. We start to meditate because we know that we can no longer live our lives with meaning unless we set out in all seriousness – and with discipline – to be open to the source of meaning found within our deepest self.

Any of us who have even the slightest inkling of what the Christian gospel is about, know that we have been created by love and for love. We know or at least we suspect that. We know, too, that love cannot be demanded. Love cannot be earned. Love is given. In Jesus it is revealed to us how great is the extent of God's love for each of us personally. Jesus himself told us that he has placed his whole love within our hearts. By meditating we do not set out to earn or to deserve God's love. We simply set out to be open to what is given, to what is.

Let me describe, as simply as possible, the way of meditation. The first thing to understand is that we must be utterly serious in devoting time to this search, to this pilgrimage. What I suggest is that you put aside time each morning and each evening. You will learn to see that time not as your own, not as time that is at your disposition, but as time that you freely consecrate to this pilgrimage so that you may enter into the total mystery of life. Do not underestimate what Jesus speaks of. Do not underestimate the call to each one of us to travel with him into the infinite mystery of God's love.

That is the call to Christians. So, the first thing you need is the time every morning and evening for the practice of meditation. What do you do in these times? All that is required is that we sit as still as possible. Meditation is a total commitment and involvement in the mystery of God, body and spirit as totally available to God as we can make them in this life. We need stillness of body and spirit to find a real sense of the harmony that we ourselves *are*, so that we may enter into a fully harmonious relationship with God. So learn to sit as still as you can. It is a discipline and a challenge but it is necessary. Then close your eyes lightly and begin to recite your word or your phrase. Do not say any prayers but allow the prayer of Christ to emerge within your own heart. Do not seek to imagine a God who is absent or distant but rather seek to be open to the God who is present in your heart.

Meditating is sometimes called the 'prayer of faith' because we seek to leave self behind and to be open to the powerful, personal presence of Christ in our hearts. The word that we say, our mantra, is like the sacrament, the outward sign of our faith in his presence. You have to learn this. On the way you will find distractions, endless thoughts coming into your mind. Do not use any energy trying to dispel them. Use all your energy to stay gently and faithfully with the recitation of your word. Let me remind you again: to meditate it is necessary to say the word from the beginning to the end.

If you are going to meditate now, after reading this, in order to forget all these words that I have been using you could play a little music or just be silent. Allow a few moments to take you beyond words.

Or listen to these words of St Paul writing to the Corinthians. He is speaking to people who are finding it difficult to understand the gospel:

> Their unbelieving minds are so blinded by the God of this passing age, that the gospel of the glory of Christ, who is the very image of God, cannot dawn upon them and bring them light. It is not ourselves that we proclaim: we proclaim Christ Jesus as Lord, and ourselves as your servants, for the sake of Jesus. For the same God who said, 'Out of darkness let light shine', has caused his light to shine within us, to give the light of revelation – the revelation of the glory of God in the face of Jesus Christ. (2 Cor. 4.4–6)

The light and the glory are to be found in our own hearts. Let us set out together on the path to that light, to that glory.

4

Total Potential

In meditation it is very important to realize that we do not set out on the path with just limited goals. We set out to realize our total potential. We are not just seeking immediate, limited goals. For example, we are not just learning to concentrate. We are not just learning to be silent, to relax, or to be still or calm. Meditation is often described as the way of self-realization. But that means realizing our *total* capacity for life. In other words, we are seeking to go from the periphery of limited goals to the centre, to the heart of realization.

Therefore, the journey involves our total being. This is the challenge. It is a challenge that everybody who starts out on this journey should understand at the beginning of the journey. Every part of our personality and every aspect of our life must be brought into this exercise. Then, every part of our personality and every part of our life has to be transcended as we journey from the periphery to the centre. Our family life, all our relationships, our work, our recreation – everything in our life is brought into harmony because in the process of meditation everything in our life is aligned on the centre. So we must understand that a profound commitment to the spiritual reality has repercussions in our total life.

We have, of course, to begin and we have to begin with confidence. Begin by knowing that the demand is profound *because* the journey is profound. The journey demands courage, energy and dedication. It demands all these three things.

But what we have to do first is to commit ourselves to the first step. The way to the centre is the way of our daily meditation, the time we set aside every morning and every evening of our life.

As Christians we believe that the source of all energy, of all harmony, is to be found in our hearts. The practice of meditation is simply the way to be open to this presence, to this energy, to this harmony, and to be open to it ever more profoundly. As we unite ourselves with this source of energy and harmony we ourselves are energized and made harmonious. But the harmony and the energy are infinite. That is why we give our total attention to saying the mantra, to saying our word. We give our total attention and total dedication to our times of meditation twice daily. The power for this journey comes from beyond ourselves and yet it is within our own hearts. Remember that the journey, the spiritual journey, is a journey into the depths of God, into the depths of the divine mystery itself. It is a journey that asks of us only simple faith – the faith to return day after day with childlike attention to our meditation, not demanding anything, not asking for anything but simply being in the presence. At those times we seek to be still, to be silent, so that we may leave the periphery and return to the centre.

Let me describe again the way of meditation. In saying the word, you enter a great tradition, a tradition of men and women who have meditated over the centuries. In meditating they sought to transcend their own limitations and to enter into the wonder of God, into the heart of the divine energy by entering their own heart. When we meditate we are still, body and soul, mind and spirit, entirely open to the presence of God, knowing that presence to be pure love, pure gentleness, pure forgiveness. In that presence we become who we are: creatures created by God, redeemed by the love of Jesus, creatures who are temples of the Holy Spirit. In that experience we are made utterly free, free to be ourselves, free to love ourselves, our neighbour and God.

Listen to the words of Jesus:

> If you dwell within the revelation I have brought, you are indeed my disciples; you shall know the truth, and the truth will set you free. (John 8.31–32)

The revelation Jesus has brought is that the Spirit dwells in our hearts and that this is the power, the energy that takes us to the Father. And more: 'If the Son sets you free you will indeed be free' (John 8.36).

Meditation is the leaving behind of all slavery, all addiction and ultimately of all limitations. It is an entry into the freedom of God, the freedom of the life of the Trinity. All we need do is open our hearts to that reality. The way is the way of the mantra.

5

Experience and Expansion

This is from St Paul writing to the Ephesians:

> With this in mind then I kneel in prayer to the Father,
> from whom every family in heaven and on earth takes its
> name, that out of the treasures of his glory he may grant
> you strength and power through his Spirit in your inner
> being, that through faith Christ may dwell in your hearts
> in love. With deep roots and firm foundations may you be
> strong to grasp, with all God's people, what is the breadth
> and length and height and depth of the love of Christ, and
> to know it, though it is beyond knowledge. So may you
> attain to fullness of being, the fullness of God himself.
> (Eph. 3.14–19)

This is what Christianity is about: experiencing the power
of God in our own hearts and expanding in Spirit so that
we expand into the fullness of God himself. The great religious question facing us all is how can we really enter into
this as something that is utterly real for each of us? It is not
enough just to admire the language or the ideas or the theology. We have to know that this is a destiny to which each
of us is summoned, not content to lead our lives just on a
two-dimensional plane but to make profound contact with
our own spirit. And then we are led through into the Spirit
of God.

Christian meditation is not just about centring ourselves on ourselves. It is true that the first task for each person is to make contact with his or her own centre, but that is only the first step. We must go beyond that into the limitless freedom of union with God. That is what our faith is about: limitless freedom as we soar beyond ourselves into the mystery, the infinite mystery, of God.

When we first hear about meditation we can easily become excited, even intoxicated by it. Then we begin to meditate and practise and *then* we begin to realize the infinity of the mystery. At that stage we can easily become frightened or perturbed. But the essential proclamation of Jesus is that the infinite mystery is a mystery of infinite gentleness, of infinite love. When we begin to understand that, we realize with an even greater sense of urgency why we cannot refrain from entering into the great power source, or from opening ourselves to the source of all energy, the source who is God.

Everything depends on the practice. It is not enough to read books about meditation. The fewer books you read about it the better. It is not enough to admire it from a distance. What is essential is that each of us, wherever we are on the pilgrimage, whether we have been meditating for a week or a decade always go back to the beginning. In this way we tread the pilgrimage humbly, faithfully and lovingly. Meditation is utter simplicity. You can tell a six-year-old child how to meditate in about two minutes. It is the simplicity that poses the greatest challenge to us.

When you meditate try to be as still as possible, to *sit still*. As you prepare to meditate, take a few moments to find a comfortable posture. The only essential rule is that you sit as upright as you can. When you are sitting still, close your eyes gently and spend a couple of minutes just becoming calm. You could breathe fairly deeply for a few breaths while you settle yourself down. Then begin to say your word. Meditation is not about analysis. It is about a total synthesis. That is often a problem for us because, for much of our life, we live as though we had a television monitor screen beside us; we are always looking at it to see how we are feeling, what we are thinking, what our reactions are. But in meditating we learn to turn the television monitor off. We learn to be. The way of learning is saying the mantra. Just to recite it is to learn this.

It would almost be impossible for you not to feel, when you begin, 'Surely this is a great waste of time. Shouldn't I be using this marvellous mind that the Lord has given me, this wonderful intelligence that I have . . . and so forth . . . to deepen my insights and understanding?' But you need to learn to be still. You need to learn, from your own experience, what St John of the Cross meant when he wrote: 'The way of possession is the way of dispossession.' The great expression that the early monks used to describe the way of meditation was that it was the way of poverty. We dispossess ourselves of all our words, of all our ideas; and we learn to be utterly still.

'Out of the treasures of His glory, may He grant you strength and power through His Spirit in your inner being, that through faith Christ may dwell in your hearts in love.' Meditation is a journey to your own heart; first, to find your own heart, your own being and then to make the greatest discovery that it is possible for any human being to make: that the Lord Jesus dwells in your heart in love. Making that discovery is to be transformed, transfigured, by entering into what St Paul could only describe as a 'new creation'. Fullness of being, the fullness of God himself is the only 'end' of our meditation.

Never forget the importance of the simplicity of your approach to meditation. It does not matter how long we have been meditating, each of us must try every day to meditate every morning and every evening. The minimum time is about twenty minutes; the optimum time about thirty. All you have to learn to do is to say your mantra, your word, from the beginning to the end of each meditation.

Ma ra na tha

Leave the rest to God. Everything beyond that is gift. We do not go to meditation with any demands. Essentially we go to meditate because we know there is only the going. There is only the way. To be on the way is the only ultimately important thing. Do not be discouraged when you find you are not saying your mantra. Return to it. Do not be discouraged if you find you miss one of your meditations or if you give up the practice for a while. Return to it. Always remember there is only the way: the way to God.

'So may you attain to fullness of being, the fullness of God himself.' (Eph. 3.19)

6

Purity of Heart

The most important thing that anyone could discover is the extent of our own potential. In the Christian revelation, that potential is infinite. Another way of saying this is that our destiny is to be expanded beyond ourselves into infinity. But not just into a nameless infinity, because it means to travel into God who is love. We need to understand that for this journey, for this expansion, we must be purified.

'Blessed are the pure in heart for they shall see God' (Matt. 5.8). 'Pure in heart': all of us are called to this form of purity. St Paul, writing to the Ephesians, says: 'I pray that your inward eyes may be illumined' (Eph. 1.18). This is our task of purity: our *inward eyes* must be opened. We must not be content to lead our lives on the surface or to be wholly absorbed by what is passing away. Our inward eyes must be opened, 'so that you know the wealth and the glory of the share he offers you' (Eph. 1.18). So often, we seem content to live our lives in darkness and confusion, not knowing clearly where we are or where we are going. In us, darkness results not from any darkness of God but simply because our inward eyes are closed. As long as the inward eye is closed we remain in the dark.

Meditation is a gentle opening of our inward eyes. It is a gentle going beyond surface, shallow living. Learning to root our lives in what is eternal, rather than in what is passing away, and what is dying, in eternal life: this is the way of meditation.

'Blessed are the pure in heart': purity is an absolutely necessary and universal quality. Purity is clarity and clarity is
clear vision, seeing what is. This means not seeing everything
in terms of myself. 'Am I enjoying myself? Am I growing?
Am I getting anything out of this? Will this make me more
fulfilled?' We come to understand that God is the centre of
our soul, of our being. The clarity we require is to see what
is in itself. Meditation brings us to the clarity to see that
God is. To see God we must be pure in heart. So, we must
be purified. We must transcend our self-centred desire. We
must learn to be free, not to be enchained to images, illusions and desires. Free to open our inward eyes without fear,
with love, so that we may see love.

Meditation is the way to this seeing. There is nothing
dramatic about meditation. Most important in learning to
meditate is to understand its absolute ordinariness. There
is nothing theatrical about it. It is absolutely ordinary. The
next most important thing is to start. Do not ask yourself:
'Have I the resources for the journey, the necessary will
power, strength of character or . . . whatever?' Only begin.

Once you begin, everything you need for the journey is
given to you.

To begin, build your meditation into every day. It is
impossible to learn to meditate without meditating. So put
in the time, every morning and evening. Meditating is like
breathing. You do not, strictly speaking, breathe for what
you are going to get out of it. But breathing is necessary for
living. If we want to enter into the invitation given us by
Jesus, that our inward eyes be illumined, so that we come to
enter the wealth and glory of the gift of God in Jesus, that's
why we learn to say our word.

To meditate all you have to learn to do is to say your mantra. Breathing in, we breathe in the power of God. Breathing
out, we breathe out our love, into his hands. It is the actual

experience of meditation – the stillness of body, the grow-ing stillness of mind – that brings us into a state of total empathy with God. Do not be worried by your distractions. Do not rate yourself for success. Say your mantra and be content to say it and continue to say it.

Very important to understand when you are beginning is *why* you say your mantra from the beginning to the end of your meditation. Do not float. Don't allow yourself just to rest on your oars. Say your mantra and keep saying it in the face of distraction. Do not use any energy to try to dispel the distraction. Use all your energy to say your mantra with absolute gentleness, with absolute fidelity. The only thing you need bother about is being. Being yourself and being in God.

Reflect again, before, but not during, meditation on St Paul's words:

> I pray that the God of our Lord Jesus Christ, the all-glorious Father, may give you the spiritual powers of wisdom and vision, by which there comes the knowledge of him. I pray that your inward eyes may be illumined, so that you may know what is the hope to which he calls you, what the wealth and glory of the share he offers you among his people in their heritage and how vast the resources of his power open to us who trust in him. They are measured by his strength and might which he exerted in Christ when he raised him from the dead. (Eph. 1.17–20)

This is the destiny that we are all summoned to. The way is the way of simplicity, of openness, purity and faithfulness. The mantra, the saying of the mantra, leads us to that clear vision where we can see utterly beyond ourselves. We see what is. We know, in our own hearts, that God is and that God is love.

7

Our Two Lives

Today we have got used to speaking about our inner or spiritual life and our outer or secular life. But, if we are to understand what Christianity is about, it is above all about a harmonious life, a life that is beyond all divisions.

It is a life where inner life and outer are always in harmony, always in a state of free-flow. But it is important to understand that all significant growth starts from the interior. Essential personal growth begins in the deepest centre of our being and then grows outward. The harmony that exists when this level of growth takes place is not just between our inner and outer lives, although this is something of no small importance. It is also a harmony with all creation. The reason, in that vision of Jesus which he proclaims and calls upon us to realize and to proclaim in our turn, is that the point where we begin this essential growth is God, and 'God', as St John of the Cross puts it, 'is the centre of my soul'.

The value of meditation is that it is a journey to this state of peace, harmony and purity, where we discover ourselves springing from the creative hand of God. That experience is foundational for us. It is an experience that gives a perspective on the whole of life. So meditation is also the great way of integration. The lesson we have to learn is that *being* is prior to *doing*. Unless we learn who we are, we will never come to authentic personhood. In the growing simplicity of

meditation we discover, we experience, our unique personhood and we make this discovery because we lose our false
ego. We leave behind all the images we have about ourselves
or imagine that others have of us.

In laying down all these masks and by learning to be content simply to be who we are, we find a profound sense of
peace and rest. But perhaps the greatest gift in meditation is
that once we enter into this realm of reality all our experience *is* our own experience. We no longer live vicariously.
We don't live our lives with pre-programmed responses. Our
experience is what we might call 'primary experience', not
experience always apprehended second-hand. The way of
meditation is the way of tending and caring for our essential
being – body and soul. Meditation itself, as we enter into it,
is an experience of the total unity of body and spirit, alive
from the centre and not just in contact with a second-hand
reality at the extremities.

We gradually come to see what it means, in the Christian
understanding, when we say that we are alive with the life of
Christ. It is an experience of the total unity of body and spirit.
And so the first thing each of us must learn in meditation is
to sit still. Our body peaceful, silent and still: this is the only
essential rule of posture. The mantra then is just like the bleep
that guides an aircraft into the airport in fog. You listen to
it, you attend to it and you travel with it to the centre. Often
you will have the feeling of peacefulness and you will feel like
resting and saying, 'This is it, I have now gone beyond the
need to say the mantra.' Resist that temptation and say your
mantra from the beginning to the end (*ma ra na tha*).

Let go of your thoughts, of all your imagination. You will
find that for some time they will invade your consciousness.
The only thing to do is to learn to say your mantra, to recite
it, to sound it gently, while the distractions are there. Do
not use energy to dispel distraction. Use all your energy just

to listen to the sound of the mantra. To learn to meditate it is then necessary to build it in as part of the daily fabric of your life. Approach your times of meditation with a certain discipline. Choose a regular time. It is this discipline that sets us free to be the unique person we are called to *be*, to be in a state of union with God. Unity of body and spirit, union *with* God. On the way to that state we have to learn to be free. The discipline of meditation leads us to this state where we can accept totally the free gift of our own being from God's hand.

Meditation is learning to be alive, from the centre of your being, in every part of your being. Listen to these words of the first letter of John:

> It was there from the beginning; we have heard it; we have seen it with our own eyes; we looked upon it, and felt it with our own hands; and it is of this that we tell. Our theme is the word of life. This life was made visible; we have seen it and bear our testimony; we here declare to you the eternal life which dwelt with the Father and was made visible to us. What we have seen and heard we declare to you, so that you and we together may share in a common life, that life which we share with the Father and his Son Jesus Christ. And we write this in order that the joy of us all may be complete. (1 John 1.1–4)

Meditation is about this: entering into and sharing that common life, the life that we share with the Father and his Son in the Spirit.

8

Heart-Longing

Recently I was reading an article by a Russian holy man who gives his opinion that in the heart of everyone there is a longing for *something*. It is not always clearly understood, and he says that sometimes this heart-longing is like an ache, a deep aching in the heart. He says that this longing and ache is there to fill the heart with infinity.

The longing, he says, is the longing that everyone has, to penetrate beyond time and space into what is eternal. This is the capacity that all men and woman have and yet, so often, the longing for it remains just a longing, the ache remains just an ache, because they don't know how to go beyond. This is what the tradition of prayer is for. The tradition is a way to go beyond the limitations of our life, all the limitations of our being, and to find our meaning and our place: to find out not only *who* we are but *where* we should be. The Russian abbot says that the only place we can truly be is in the light of God. The light that shines in our hearts. He says the principal task of every life is to allow that light to shine with brilliant clarity. This is exactly the purpose of Christian meditation. I would like to try to explain, in so far as I can, what the practice of Christian meditation is about and why it has such importance.

If you are just beginning to meditate I want to explain, first of all, that to meditate is simplicity itself. All you have to do is faithfully to say your word. If you can once see the importance of opening your heart to this light, of understanding where you are and who you are in the light of God, then you will say your word every morning and every evening for the rest of your life. Your morning meditation will be a preparation for your day. It will send you into the day with that light released, shining in your heart. More and more you will see your day with that light. In the evening when you come home from work or study you will bring your day together, and understand it in that same light. Remember the light is the light of God which shines in everyone's heart if only we could realize it. And pure prayer, meditation, is the way to realize that this light is the supreme reality.

Sometimes, people ask, 'How could I possibly just say this one word for a whole half an hour?' Or even perhaps they will ask more pointedly, 'How could I say it daily for twenty years, or for the rest of my life?' When people first hear about meditation and even when they begin to practise it, they wonder, 'Is this going to be excruciatingly boring?' But saying the mantra is just like setting up the rhythm of a poem. A poem depends upon metre and rhythm, and sometimes rhyme, which is continually sounded throughout the poem to give it its special character; through the poet's craft all this helps to come to the insight and meaning that the poem communicates through the words. Meditation is like that. The mantra grounds you, roots you, in the rhythm of God, in the metre of God, in the idiom of God. It is when you are rooted and grounded in that experience, rhyming with God, that insight, understanding and awareness come to you. The awareness is simply that you are, the awareness is that God is.

The awareness comes through the ordinary experience of your daily sitting down to meditate. If you want to learn to meditate, to ground and root your life in God, you will need to understand how utterly ordinary your meditation is. It is not the time when you just go in for some spirituality. It is the time when the essential you is most essentially you. That is the power of meditation, and the power of the mantra is that it establishes this rhythm in your life and so grounds your life in God.

The purpose of all spirituality, and of all religion, is that we should be anchored in God. Another way of saying this is that we should be anchored in supreme, absolute reality. The real danger that we have to avoid is living on the basis of illusion, of thinking that the illusions are real. This is why we have to be anchored in God, so that we can judge everything with his eternal insight that we call wisdom: knowing what is real, knowing what is false, knowing what endures, knowing what passes away. Rooting our lives here and now in what endures, in what is eternal, means that we become more real and that we are even now *in the present*, living our lives from eternal truth, in eternal reality.

Remember the simplicity and the ordinariness of the practice. It is no good just talking about God. It is no good just talking about spirituality. You can read all the books on Zen Buddhism and all the commentaries on the Upanishads but without the practice you will have achieved very little. You can read the New Testament from beginning to end and all the commentaries on it. But without the practice and without the experience that motivated the people who wrote it you will make very little contact with its meaning.

Our morning and evening meditations are a commitment to what is true, real, and genuinely important. The mantra is like the rhythm and metre of the poem; and, as you meditate, the infinite variety that is God will sustain and delight you. But we have to begin by mastering the metre and the rhythm, and the first task of anyone who wants to learn how to meditate is to root your word, your mantra, in your heart.

Listen to what St Peter has to say about the context in which we live our lives:

> His divine power has bestowed on us everything that makes for life and true religion, enabling us to know the One who called us by his own splendour and might. (2 Pet. 1.3)

He continues by saying that the invitation that is given to each one of us is to 'share in the very being of God'. That is the invitation. To accept it, all we have to do is to set out on the pilgrimage which is, in the first place, to our own heart. There we find the light, the courage and the love that will then take us beyond and into the infinite wisdom and love of God.

9

Wholly Present

There are lots of books on why to meditate. There are lots of books about what happens when you meditate. But the most important thing is to be absolutely clear about how to meditate. And then, to meditate every day – every morning and every evening.

Meditation is a way of becoming wholly present to the now, to the present moment. When we meditate, each of us has to try to forget ourselves as we learn to say our word, our mantra, with complete concentration and self-forgetfulness. The snare that prevents us from becoming free is nothing else than self-consciousness. The call that each of us has to follow, therefore, is to become *wholly* conscious.

Perhaps most of us spend so much of our time thinking about the past or planning for the future that there is a very real danger that we never fully come to terms with the present. I am sure you know how painful it is to be with someone who is always living in the past; and it is equally painful to be with someone who is always thinking of the future. To meditate we need to learn to be wholly attentive in the present to our mantra, to listen to it with simplicity of spirit and with concentration. When we meditate we are not thinking about the past at all. In a real sense, we have become freed from the past. For religious people this is important, so that we are not thinking about a man called Jesus who lived in the past. That is not where we *are*. We are wholly in the *present* and, as we shall see, in religious terms this means being wholly present to the living Christ. We are freed from the past because, as we meditate, as we open ourselves to the power of the living Christ, we see that, because of the reality of what is now, in the present, the past has no ultimate power over us.

One of the problems in learning to meditate is that we have to become humble by letting go of all the ways that the past controls us as well as the ways we try to control the future. When we meditate we are not trying to make the present happen. We are not trying to make anything happen. The present is. We are not trying to conjure up God or God's power or the Spirit. God is. It is all important to know that when we meditate we are simply being open to the present, to what is.

People often ask, 'How long do I have to meditate before something happens?' The only answer to that question is, 'Just as long as it takes us to be wholly committed to the present moment, to what is.' That is the challenge and so, if you find yourself asking, 'How long is this going to take?', the word to remember is *commitment*.

Commit yourself to say your mantra – with a total commitment. You cannot meditate with one foot on the shore. You have to launch out into the deep. You have to say your mantra with a real sense of abandon. In other words, you have to be as fully open as you can to the Spirit in your heart, without reservation, without conditions. Don't ask yourself, 'What will this demand of me? What will it lead me to?' All of us must go where we are led and answer the summons that calls us to be who we are in the presence of the God who is. That is the great challenge.

Just as we are freed from the past, so we are free of the future. In that very moment when we realize that what is, is sufficient, for now, forever, we have touched eternity. So the question that arises is, 'What is?' To say that 'God is' would be enough. But the power of the Christian revelation consists in its multi-dimensional proclamation that God not only is, he is now, he is here, he is always, he is in our hearts, he is love.

Wisdom, in the Christian vision, consists in having this truth sharply in focus. It consists in knowing this with utter certainty and in living from the power of its truth with every ounce of our energy and in every fibre of our being. It consists, too, in the willingness to be transformed by that power, taken out of and beyond ourselves into the very heart of the mystery itself.

Christian meditation is the process whereby we reduce ourselves to that point of nothingness that allows this truth to enter us, to become wholly real for us. It is important for all of us to know that we are not meant to construct our own reality. We are simply trying to enter whole-heartedly into what is.

When we meditate, we must remember to sit as still as we can. Our stillness is the outward sign of the abandonment of self. By sitting still, our body and our spirit become one in the stillness. Take a few moments at the beginning to find a comfortable sitting posture. Take two or three deep breaths so that you can calm yourself externally. And then for the entire time of the meditation say your word. The word I recommend to lead you to abandonment, to deep silence, to God, is *maranatha*.

Remember only that God is. God is here. God is now. God is in my heart. God is love. The requirements are stillness, awareness, simplicity, commitment, discipline. Sit still. Say the word from the beginning to the end. The mantra is the way.

If you are going to meditate now after reading this you could prepare for this stillness and listen to St Paul:

Finally then, find your strength in the Lord, in his mighty power. Give yourselves wholly to prayer and entreaty; pray on every occasion in the power of the Spirit . . . Whatever you do put your whole heart into it as if you were doing it for the Lord and not for men . . . for Christ is the master. (Eph. 6.18; Col. 3.23–24)

IO

Questions

QUESTION: Are we supposed to be aware of our breathing or be concentrating only on the mantra?

RESPONSE: When you begin, it is hardly possible to meditate without being rather self-conscious about the whole process, because it is something we are not used to. But I think breathing while you are meditating is like breathing at all other times. You breathe in order to keep going and you are not usually very conscious about it.

When you begin to say your mantra and breathe at the same time you become more conscious about the breathing just as you do of yourself sitting still, meditating and saying your mantra.

You could say the mantra as you breathe in and breathe out in silence. Or you could say the first two syllables (ma ra) as you breathe in and the next two (na tha) as you breathe out. There is no strict rule about it. Remember the whole thing is one and simple. Keep your whole attention on the mantra and don't divide it between the mantra and the breath. The whole purpose of saying the mantra, on a daily basis morning and evening, is that you build it in to all your natural systems, so that it eventually becomes a wholly unself-conscious process. So, in that sense, you forget that you are meditating.

The important thing is to 'root' the mantra in your heart. Once it is rooted there, you breathe it in and breathe out in silence, quite unself-consciously.

QUESTION: Is there a point at which you give up saying your mantra?

RESPONSE: There is no point where you *give up* saying it. There is a point when you *cease* to say it. I don't recommend that you think too much about that when you are beginning; again one should not be self-conscious about it. Never be trying to make anything happen.

But basically speaking, the process is: You say your mantra every morning and every evening – for about twenty years, more or less! Then, one morning or one evening, you are aware that you are not saying your mantra. As soon as you are aware that you are not saying it, you start saying it again. Those times of 'not' saying the mantra might be a split second, or a few minutes, or the whole half-hour. But if you are aware for the whole half-hour that you have not been saying your mantra, you can be sure that you are not meditating.

A really important principle to get clear in the beginning is: 'Say your mantra until you can no longer say it.' As soon as you are aware that you are not saying it, start saying it again. The ancient monastic tradition expressed this by saying: 'The monk who knows that he is praying is not truly praying. The monk who does not know he is praying, is truly praying.'

Does that help? It is very difficult to understand this apart from or outside the experience of it; but the theology of it is very clear. The theology is that *the* prayer is the prayer of Jesus; and we have to stand back and allow his prayer full power within us.

That is the problem with commitment. A lot of people raise the question, 'Are there many ways of prayer? Is there a Buddhist way, a Hindu way, a Carmelite way, a Jesuit way . . . or whatever?' If you indulge yourself with this multiplicity, to the extent that you always say, 'Of course, there are lots of ways', then you never have to commit yourself to one way and one way is *the* way. As soon as you realize that *the* way is the prayer of Jesus, the way you are following becomes *the* way. Then your only challenge is to stand back sufficiently enough to allow his prayer to become supreme.

People say, 'If you are saying the mantra all the time, how are you going to listen to Jesus praying?' Are you 'blocking the Spirit'? But you are not listening to it at all. You are being launched into that prayer. It is very difficult to talk about it without using images, but the prayer of Jesus is like a rushing torrent flowing between Jesus and the Father. What we have to do is to plunge ourselves into that and be swept along by it. It is a torrent of love, not a torrent of words or images. And that is why we need to learn to be wholly silent. The mantra is simply bringing us deeper and deeper into that silence.

QUESTION: How long should each meditation last?
RESPONSE: I would recommend the minimum time as twenty minutes. The optimum and, I would suggest, the maximum time is half an hour. I would not recommend anyone who is beginning to meditate less than twenty minutes or more than thirty minutes. It is very useful to take a precise time slot and say, 'I am going to meditate now for twenty minutes', and when the twenty minutes is up, to end the meditation. The temptation is, when the meditation is going well, to prolong it and when it is going badly, to shorten it. The really important thing is to step out of that self-consciousness and work to a disciplined limit. The discipline of meditation is of great importance.

QUESTION: Fr John, I remember you saying once that you did not recommend meditating in the late evening. One of the reasons was that it made one so alert that you simply could just not go to sleep afterwards. To my shame I must report that I have exactly the opposite difficulty. If I meditate late in the day my difficulty is to stay awake. I wonder if you have any suggestions. Even if I do it at six o'clock I have trouble staying awake. Do you have any suggestions about the art of staying alert?

RESPONSE: This is a perennial problem. It is particularly acute when you are starting to meditate. But all of us who have been meditating for years, if we have not enough oxygen or don't get enough sleep will fall asleep.

The simple rules are: to meditate in a place that is not over-heated and is well aired. Many people who come to meditate with us complain that the room is under-heated, particularly our upstairs meditation room; but that may be a helpful part of the process of keeping awake.

For example, if you meditate early in the evening and if you tend regularly to fall asleep it might be a wise idea to take a nap for ten minutes or so before you meditate.

You could also try a very simple relaxation exercise by lying flat on the floor. Allow the floor to take the full weight of your body by relaxing each of your legs and areas of your body section by section, just sinking into the floor, as it were. But we are not used to being completely relaxed and completely alert at the same time. And so, as we have to be completely relaxed when meditating, when we do relax we think, 'Aha, all systems are being shut down; I am getting relaxed; this is a sign I must go to sleep.' And the body becomes drowsy or goes to sleep. The reverse is true too. Nobody goes to sleep when they are playing a game of squash, because the adrenalin is pumping around and you are totally alert.

In meditating you want to develop the capacity to be as relaxed as at the moment just before you go to sleep and yet as awake as though you were playing a game of squash. That is something we have to learn. You need to be very patient about it.

Apart from those simple rules of a good air supply, loose clothing, not too warm, not meditating just after a big meal, I often recommend people to wash their face with cold water just before meditating. It might even be a good idea to have a cold shower! These simple practical rules are the best ones to observe. And, of course, adequate exercise, adequate rest and adequate sleep every day.

11

The School of Cassian

Meditation has a special place in the monastic tradition. The school of teaching that we follow is that of John Cassian, who represented the teaching of the very earliest monastic fathers. He was teaching a tradition that depended on the essential human quality of fidelity and he saw daily practice as the essence of that fidelity.

When we look at meditation we have to be very careful not to be taken in by mere techniques. The essence of meditation is not technique but what John Cassian called 'purity of heart'. In his conferences he says that the essence and the purpose of meditation is the Kingdom of God; that is, God's power released and having full sway in our hearts. But then he goes on to say that before we can achieve this ultimate aim we have to undergo a preliminary stage. The preliminary step to this he calls purity of heart. The aim of all meditation is to purify our heart. In modern language we could describe this as to 'clarify consciousness'.

We must beware of thinking that we can do this merely by the use of techniques. The method is important but our approach to it is more important. We approach it in a simple, human fashion that recognizes purity of heart as simply the first step we take. We are used to looking for techniques that produce instant results. The tradition we speak from is neither a technique-oriented nor an instant-result tradition.

Our school, of which John Cassian was the great teacher, is one of infinite gentleness and patience and total fidelity.

In the nineteenth century, a great writer on the spiritual life called Theophane the Recluse went so far as to say that unless we can come to this purity of heart that he calls 'attention', by learning to attend and to be present, we will never understand the gentleness of Christ, or his 'blessedness' or the power of his resurrection. So the first thing to understand when you come to think about Christian meditation is the work of attention, its simplicity and humanness. Purity of heart, 'clarity of consciousness', is learning through attention to see clearly. So often our vision is clouded by our egoism or desire. So often we see others in terms of their usefulness to us or how they can serve our needs: 'What will they do for me?'

In so far as we see others like this we do not see them clearly, as they are. And if we do not see them as they are, we cannot love them. Again, that is the whole purpose of our Christian commitment, the final goal of the Kingdom of God which is the vision of God, which is love. The Kingdom of God is simply that state in which we all together live directly from God's power. We live from his power of love, within the ambiance of his love; and this communicates and expands his love in our hearts, in our lives, in all our relationships.

The first step, however, is purity of heart. Coming to it involves what the author of the *Cloud of Unknowing* calls 'loosening the root of sin within us'. Another way of putting that is learning to be free, learning to live out of the infinite liberty of God and not to be constrained by our own possessiveness, our own desire and selfishness. This is the high road to liberty and to joy: not to try to dominate one another, or to impress one another, but to love one another. This is where the *joy* of the Christian vision of reality comes from.

The method that we have from John Cassian, and from the *Cloud of Unknowing* a thousand years later, is very simple.

To meditate every day, every morning and every evening. The time: a minimum when you start of about twenty minutes and the optimum time about half an hour. My advice is to choose a set period of time, twenty minutes, twenty-five or half an hour, and stick to it. Do not meditate longer when your meditation is going well or shorter when it is going badly. Stick to the set time, twenty, twenty-five or thirty minutes. You need to be very practical about it. So, find a way of measuring the time so you are not glancing at your watch every five minutes saying, 'Surely it must be over by now!' During the meditation you have to learn to do one thing: to say your mantra.

The mantra is a word or short phrase; you learn simply to recite it from the beginning to the end of each meditation. When you start, it is difficult to see that it is this discipline of the word itself that is so important and that fidelity is the way to freedom. Recite the word, paying attention to it and leaving behind your own thoughts, desires, your own feelings, including your imagination. The essence of meditation is to stop thinking about yourself and to listen to the word. The difficulty of this is that it reduces you down to a zero point and then you want to think about yourself. You may want to ask, 'Am I making progress? Am I getting nearer to enlightenment? Is this actually working?' But you must abandon all those thoughts and then take it on faith that it is being reduced to *and* beyond that zero point that will take you through to the other side, into the infinity of God's love. But you do at first have to take it on faith that it is the daily return, every morning and every evening, to the recitation of that word in absolute faith and fidelity that will gradually bring you to that point of pure nothingness. It is at that point of pure nothingness that you enter into the mystery of God.

The process is important and when you are beginning it is important, too, that you understand the simplicity of it. It is important, for example, to sit still. When you meditate take a couple of moments to become really comfortable in your posture. The only essential rule is to sit as upright as you can and then sit as still as you can. It is difficult when you begin. Religious people are likely to get very 'holy' thoughts and these seem to be thoughts that should be followed. Let them go. For those who are not so religious, they may get 'unholy' thoughts. Let them go, too. Listen to the word and devote your whole attention to it. When you begin you have to take that on faith. Remember the simple purpose is to stop thinking about yourself.

Meditation is a state of absolute union and harmony between body and spirit. The body becomes, as it were, an external symbol for the interior stillness that comes. Close your eyes gently and then begin to recite your word. Do not bother too much about breathing techniques – or any technique – just say it. Everything else will fall into position later. When you find – as you certainly will find when you begin – that you have stopped saying the word or that you are thinking about something else, come back to it gently. To learn to meditate all you have to do is to return to the practice every morning and every evening. What you will then discover is what we are promised in the Christian revelation: that this transcending of self leads you right into the heart of the life of God.

The Christian meditator is therefore able to understand with deeper personal meaning these words of St Paul writing to the Romans:

Therefore, I implore you by God's mercy to offer your very selves to him: a living sacrifice, dedicated and fit for his acceptance, the worship offered by mind and heart. Adapt yourselves no longer to the pattern of this present world, but let your minds be remade and your whole nature thus transformed. Then you will be able to discern the will of God, and to know what is good, acceptable and perfect. (Rom. 12.1–2)

That is what meditation is about: allowing our minds to be remade and our whole nature thus transformed.

The Delicate Balance

These are words of Jesus recorded in the Gospel of Luke:

> If anyone wishes to be a follower of mine he must leave
> self behind. Day after day he must take up his cross and
> follow me. Whoever cares for his own safety is lost. But
> if a person will let himself be lost for my sake that one is
> safe. (Luke 9.23–25)

For us the big problem in trying to understand the gospel is
to understand its paradox. If we want to find our lives we
must be prepared to lose them. Somehow or other – if we
want to come to the truth – each of us must find that delicate balance between self-abandonment and self-fulfilment.
The balance is of great importance because if we go solely
for self-fulfilment we are likely to become an insufferable
person, seeing everything, all reality, all relationships, only
in terms of our own self-fulfilment. If, on the other hand,
we go only for self-abandonment we are likely to be equally
insufferable too, seeing ourselves as martyrs and constantly
denying our life.

Jesus is talking about a balance: self-abandonment *and*
self-fulfilment. And so we have to discover within ourselves
that delicate point of balance. It might be described as the
point of pure consciousness within each person. It is a delicate place of balance. Here we discover true equilibrium:

neither totally committed to abandonment, nor totally committed to fulfilment, but totally committed to absolute reality. If we are totally committed to abandonment we are committed to abandoning ourselves. If we are totally committed to fulfilment we are committed to fulfilment for ourselves. But the point of pure consciousness within us is directed infinitely beyond ourselves, and we find ourselves by transcendence.

Just think for a moment about desire. Jesus says, 'Set your minds first on the Kingdom of God.' All of us would like to set our minds on the Kingdom of God, but unfortunately our minds are set on all sorts of other intermediate desires. We may even say that we do set our minds on the Kingdom of God. The truth is that the moment we do so – and go beyond all intermediate desire and desire only God – that is the moment of enlightenment when we pass beyond desire into the reality. The curious thing about abandonment and fulfilment is there is no fulfilment without abandonment.

We know from our own experience that the great problem is to allow ourselves to be loved. It is only when we allow ourselves to be loved that we ourselves can love. The big problem in every human life, therefore, is taking this first step of allowing oneself to be loved. *This* is abandonment. *This* is leaving self behind. This is transcending self.

What follows is love. *This* is fulfilment. *This* is the absolute discovery of self, in the other, beyond oneself. The point of balance is the point of pure consciousness. Meditation is the way by which we gently move to that point of pure consciousness, the balance that enables us to abandon *and* to find ourselves. There is only one way of learning to meditate and that is to meditate. Don't be entranced by the philosophies of meditation or by the wisdom of the sages down the ages. The most important thing is to understand very clearly in your own mind the sheer simplicity of meditation.

We are going to meditate together in a few moments and, when we do, all we have to do is to learn to say our word, our mantra. When we begin to meditate, first of all, sit still. Spend some time getting comfortable and then stay still. Abandon your body to the stillness and then, closing your eyes gently, begin to recite interiorly, silently, your word, your mantra: *ma ra na tha*. Leave every thought, every idea, every imagination behind and just listen to the recitation of your word: maranatha. In this way we go beyond all thoughts, all words, all ideas, and we learn to be still. You may ask, 'How long will this take?' The answer is, 'It takes only as long as it takes you to desire one thing: to set your mind on the Kingdom.'

In setting your mind on the Kingdom, as Jesus tells us, everything else is given to you, every desire is fulfilled. It does not matter how long it takes. The only thing that matters is that each of us, according to our own capacity, is on the way. That means finding the time – this probably involves a measure of sacrifice – to meditate every morning and every evening. What will you be doing during that time? Setting your mind on the Kingdom. Nothing else. It is important to understand when you begin that it is necessary to meditate every day, every morning and every evening. Do not be discouraged by failure. We all fail. No one, I think, who has ever started to meditate has not begun, stopped, begun again, stopped, given up, started again. No one, I think, who has ever meditated has not had the same experience in meditating. We begin to say our mantra and then our mind wanders off.

The important thing to understand, however, when you are meditating is to say your mantra as faithfully as you can. If you find your mind has wandered off, start again and keep coming back to it. You will learn discipline by your faithfulness and the discipline will take you beyond yourself into pure consciousness, into pure innocence, into pure love. If you give up meditating for a day, a week, a month or a year, come back to it. Start again. Your meditation will eventually take you beyond yourself into the infinite mystery of God's love.

Listen to the words of Jesus again:

If anyone wishes to be a follower of mine he must leave self behind. Day after day he must take up his cross and follow me. Whoever cares for his own safety, is lost. But if a person will let himself be lost for my sake that one is safe. (Luke 9.23–25)

PART 2

Being on the Way

13

Life as Revelation

I want to reflect now about meditation as a way that profoundly alters our whole life. As you know from your own experience, meditation is a way of silence. We have to learn to be profoundly still, profoundly silent, and that silence is both interior and exterior. This means that our interior life and our exterior life have to come together in harmony in whatever we do: how we conduct ourselves; how we handle our relationships. This is of supreme importance to the interior journey. Following the way of meditation means that everything about our life, everything interior and exterior, is a revelation: revealing God and leading us to God. In God's plan our own integrity, our own commitment, reveals the divine integrity and commitment in our life.

In the fourteenth-century the English mystic Dame Julian of Norwich described prayer as a way of complete simplicity demanding not less than everything. This is what we have to understand today. The invitation that God gives to each of us is to enter into the fullness of his life. This means that God gives us everything; but, in order to enter that fullness and receive the gift, we have to become equally generous. Everything is given, both by God *and by us*. As we begin to understand the scale of this, we can get nervous. But there is no need for fear, because it is given to us to give. The power we require to be generous is given to us, given in the silence. That is why our commitment to the silence is of such

supreme importance. The silence that we will encounter is
not just the silence of our being quiet. It is the silence of
divine energy. This is our pilgrimage. Silence is why it is so
important to learn to say the mantra.

The mantra is like a sculptor with a large block of granite. He chips away to reveal the form of the sculpture and
each time we say our mantra the form that God has for us
is being made. We may think of ourselves as slow, even as
unworthy. We may even give up saying our mantra. But the
form is there and the energy to create it is there and that
energy is the divine energy. So all we need is to return to
our practice, to our silence. Through our faithfulness the
energy flows more strongly in our heart, the silence becomes
more profound and the interior and exterior life come into
harmony.

Listen to St Paul telling us what our destiny is. We need
to listen to him with great care because so often Christians
underestimate the wonder of our vocation. We live our
Christian lives at the surface, instead of going to the profound depths.

> As scripture says of Moses, 'whenever he turns to the Lord
> the veil is removed'. Now the Lord of whom this passage
> speaks is the Spirit; and where the Spirit of the Lord is,
> there is liberty. And because for us there is no veil over
> the face, we all reflect, as in a mirror, the splendour of
> the Lord; thus we are transfigured into his likeness from
> splendour to splendour. Such is the influence of the Lord
> who is Spirit. (2 Cor. 3.16–18)

Note the words 'because for us there is no veil over the face'.
That is the power of Christian prayer. It is the power of
Christian meditation. If only we have the courage for it, the

courage, integrity and generosity to say our mantra, to lose ourselves and to find ourselves in the power of the Spirit.

The image that Jesus uses to describe this is one of immense dynamism and great power. He tries to convey to us the infinite vitality of God communicating and sharing his essence. Which is to *be*. In the chapel of New College, Oxford there is a marvellous statue by Jacob Epstein of the Raising of Lazarus from the dead. In a great mass of granite Epstein has wonderfully conveyed Lazarus bursting out of his burial clothes, the bonds of the grave. In the statue Epstein conveys something of what life is, something of the life force that is bursting out of all the chains that would hold it back. Everything that is death-dealing is defeated and Lazarus bursts back into life. He does this in the gift given to him by Jesus.

This is the essence of the life force, the creative force communicating itself, extending itself beyond all confining barriers. What we discover in our meditation is that this very same dynamism is to be found within each of us. In essence this is what the Christian proclamation is about: that we are summoned to life, abundant life, full life. And the power of life is given to us out of the immense generosity of God channelled to us through Jesus. The essence of the gospel – and this is why the gospel is 'good news' – is that this power, this vitality and creative force is to be found in our own hearts. If only we will be open to it, if only we will turn from distraction, from trivia and from what is passing away, and open the eyes of our heart to this eternal life.

But if the power is infinite, it is also infinitely gentle and compassionate. This is because the power of God is the power of love and God does not force his love upon us. He *invites* us to open our hearts to his love. He invites us to enter into the creative movement of his love. Our turning must be the same as God's. What we know – from the words and the actions of Jesus – is that God is wholly turned to us in Jesus. In our meditation, and by taking our meditation absolutely seriously, in making it the fundamental axis of our life, we make our turn.

14

Questions

QUESTION: Is there a way of sitting in the lotus position so that your feet do not fall asleep?!
RESPONSE: The answer to that is yes! The main thing is to be very patient about getting a really good sitting position. Take the best expert advice you can to learn to sit properly without impeding the blood supply and so forth. But the important thing is not the sitting position, but that you meditate. It can take a Westerner maybe a year or eighteen months to get a really good sitting posture, by the time you stretch the muscles on the thighs and so forth – and depending on how limber you are when you start. But it is better to do that outside of the meditation period, in a time for stretching, like a yoga exercise for example, rather than during meditation itself.

QUESTION: Is meditation 'quietism'?
RESPONSE: The ancient monastic word to describe the state of prayer was the Latin term '*quies*'. It contains the notion of being at rest, being in a state of silence, sometimes described as 'staying quiet in the Lord'. This state of being *in quiet* suggests complete confidence and ease at being in the presence of God. Not the same as 'quietism', which suggests an escape from reality.

In our society we are so used to striving for things, to owning things, to earning the approval of others, that it is very hard for us to think of ourselves as usefully employed if we are just 'resting in the Lord' in this state of *quies*, of being in quiet. But those of us who try to tread this pilgrimage need always to remember that just being in God's presence *is* all-sufficient. It is a form of pure action. When we are wholly present to God, we are wholly present to ourselves and wholly present to the whole of creation. But, as you know from your human experience, being wholly present to another does require ease, confidence and relaxation. You cannot have much of an up-building conversation with another person if you think the chair you are sitting in is about to collapse any moment. So being present to another requires confidence.

QUESTION: How does meditation 'spread the gospel'?
RESPONSE: 'As thou, Father, art in me, and I in thee, so also may they be in us, that the world may believe that thou didst send me' (John 17.21). These words of Jesus should remind us that prayer itself, being at prayer, in the state of prayer, is the great act of communicating the gospel. Note those words of Jesus, 'that the world may believe that thou didst send me'. The world will believe when we ourselves dwell fully in God's presence. Our meditation then is a time of ease and of quiet and it gives each of us the capacity to be at ease in all the things of God. And, in time, it gives us the ease not only to speak of the things of God, but to live our lives in Godliness.

The basic theology of meditation for the Christian is that what matters is not *my* prayer but entering into *his* prayer. In the tradition of the Church this meditation process has therefore been called the prayer of faith, contemplative prayer, pure prayer. It has been known by various names. We call it meditation, being still in the centre of our being, so that we may travel with Christ to the centre of the Trinity.

QUESTION: Is there a theology of meditation?

RESPONSE: From our experience of oneness and from our openness to the presence comes a total theology. This means a theology that arises directly from our gazing on the glory of God: our lives are shaped and reformed by this, not by our own striving, our own resolutions or our own efforts. Our lives are shaped and formed rather by the glory of God. Our meditation is simply our approach to that glory. Our way into the glory is the way of '*quies*' of quiet, of ease.

Many Christians, when they hear of the theology of meditation have questions about it. They ask, 'Is this 'quietism'? When they hear about saying the mantra, they might ask, 'Is it Pelagianism? Aren't we trying to twist God's arm by some sort of technique?' If these questions arise in your mind, or if others pose themselves to you, think of the glory of God. Saying the mantra means that we dispose ourselves; we make ourselves available. So when we come to our morning and evening meditation each day we are there, present to God, resting in his presence. But everything we know, everything is his gift: our knowledge of him, our knowledge of the way, and our knowledge of his glory.

QUESTION: Does meditation put an end to other ways of prayer?

RESPONSE: As monks we spend quite a bit of time each day at liturgical prayer. All other forms of prayer can also lead us to this pure experience of God. So meditation is not in any sense exclusive. We are not saying to anyone, 'Don't waste time saying the rosary, or your breviary.' What we are saying is, 'Enter into the pure stream of the prayer of Jesus, and launch yourself into that stream by any means you can find', whether it is the rosary, the stations of the Cross, the Divine Office, or whatever. What we say is, to enter into that stream of pure prayer you must transcend yourself, you must leave

your self behind. Learning to say your mantra and learning to
discipline yourself to this prayer every day is the way that the
tradition gives us – and our own experience reinforces this –
for journeying with Jesus and through Jesus to the Father.

Another question that often worries people is, 'What about
petitionary prayer? Is there even such a thing as petitionary
prayer? Has it any value?' Obviously there is such a thing as
petitionary prayer. Jesus himself tells us to seek so that we
will find; to ask so that we will receive. But the longer you
meditate, the more you realize that all the petitions that we
can think of are already contained in the prayer of Jesus. His
love for us and his love for the Father make him the perfect
mediator (and meditator). In the time of meditation we cast
all our cares, all our concerns totally on him; we surrender
them into his hands. Petitionary prayer is not to inform God
of what we need or what we would like. God knows already
what we need. He knows what we want.

QUESTION: I feel I am not ready – almost not worthy – to
meditate.
RESPONSE: Meditation in Christ opens us to the power of his
redemption. None of us are 'worthy' to be in his presence.
But all of us are invited by him to be in his presence. So when
we think of asking, 'Am I worthy to meditate?' we have to
think of the words of Jesus. 'Come to me all you who labour
and are overburdened and I will refresh you' (Matt. 11.28).

Our meditation is refreshment. For the time of our meditation we are relieved from the burden of thinking about
ourselves, of asking ourselves, 'Am I happy? Am I fulfilling
myself?' During the time of meditation we come into silence.
We say our mantra humbly and faithfully, and in the silence
our hearts are opened to the presence of Jesus and to his
healing love. I think none of us need really ask the question,
'Am I worthy to meditate?' All we need do is to meditate.

QUESTION: Is it important to tell others about meditation?
RESPONSE: This question came up at a day I was giving to
meditators recently: 'Do I have a responsibility to communicate meditation to others?' They were saying that they had
discovered in meditation a new dimension to their Christianity. They had found a new power and a new authority. They
had begun to read the scriptures as they had never read them
before. What was their responsibility in communicating it?

I think the answer is that once we are on the way we cannot help but communicate it. I do not think we need to be
too self-conscious about, as it were, going out of our way to
communicate meditation. I think that if we really do say our
mantra faithfully, humbly, in simplicity, every morning and
every evening, in God's good time and in his plan, we cannot
help but communicate it.

15

The Prodigal Son

Many of us are familiar with the story of The Prodigal Son: how he wanted his inheritance, went off into a foreign country, squandered it in riotous living; and then, when the country suffered a recession, he had to work as a swineherd, and all he had to eat were the husks that were given to the pigs. Then St Luke adds, 'Finally he came to his senses.'

These are important words for us because it seems that the experience of total disaster or of total poverty is necessary if we are to grow in the life of the spirit; if we are to expand and mature. It may be that there are two roads to that experience of profound poverty – the road of insight or the road of actual experience. I must say, in my own experience, that I have found it is the actual experience of deep poverty that is the really important thing.

When you have been trying to build something and it ends in disaster and failure; when you have worked at something for years only to find that the sum total, the result of the whole thing, is nothing; then you realize that the basic need for us all is to go into something much larger, much deeper than success; something more than acquiring possessions. The larger reality that becomes so much clearer is the experience of poverty. Many people come to meditation out of desperation. In facing poverty they have tried everything and nothing else seems to work.

What I want to share with you is this: the experience of poverty is only the beginning. In meditation we learn to build on our poverty and to deepen it. The great thing to understand is that the summons we have from Jesus is to follow the *way*. Not my own way but *the* way. For us as modern men and women that is very difficult to understand because almost everything in our experience prepares us to look for *my* way: what will bring me happiness, satisfaction, fulfilment. But the clear call of Jesus to each of us is to follow *the* way.

The way, as the Christian knows it, is Jesus. He is the Way, stronger than the doubts we feel: 'Is it prudent, is it possible? Is not this a reckless way of understanding your vocation or destiny?' But what we come to know is that there is only *the* way. Meditation teaches us, and strengthens us for the leap so that when the time to leap comes we hardly know that it has happened. Meditation simplifies us. Meditation gently melts away the obstacles that prevent us from leaping. It melts away our fears and does so in an entirely gentle and largely imperceptible way. It might seem to us that we are making no progress. It sometimes seems that we have been saying the mantra for weeks, months, even years with no result. When you think this, remember it is not *your* way it is *the* way. The journey we are on is not just our journey. It is *the* journey. The way is Jesus and so the way is truth and life. It is about being simple and poor:

He instructed them to take nothing for the way beyond a stick. No bread, no pack, no money in their belts. They might wear sandals but not a second coat. (Mark 6.8)

16

The Idea of Progress

People often ask, 'I don't seem to be making any progress in my meditation. What should I do about it?' Perhaps the most important progress we have to make in our meditation is to abandon the idea of making progress.

We need to understand that we are always beginning. Every time we sit down to meditate we begin again. Every meditation is a setting out; and because it is always a re-setting out it always remains fresh, always a further entry into a mystery that is infinite and inexhaustible. It is important to understand that, although we do speak of meditation as a journey, it is an unusual journey because it is a pilgrimage to purity and a way of purification. Purification can be abrasive and painful. But we must be stripped of everything that would hinder our openness to the pure energy of God. Egoism must go. Desire must go. Possessiveness must go, and that is painful. So each of us must learn to be prepared for a certain suffering involved in leaving our old ways and our old selves and becoming open to this new life, this new way of living, which is the way of God.

This should encourage us. We should take heart because the power to overcome is not only given to each of us but that power is infinite. The power that resides in the heart of each one of us to follow this way all the way, is exactly the same power that God exercised in Christ when he raised him from the dead. By accepting the discipline of meditation and by being present to ourselves and to God, every morning and evening, we open ourselves to that power. It is a vitalizing energy that is the source of all life and all love. Whatever the challenges, whatever the difficulties, whatever the suffering, this power is always with us.

Listen to St Paul, as he sets out his understanding of what the Christian life is about:

> I pray that the God of our Lord Jesus Christ, the all-glorious Father, may give you the spiritual powers of wisdom and vision by which there comes the knowledge of him. I pray that your inward eyes may be illumined so that you may know what is the hope to which he calls you and what the wealth and glory of the share he offers you and how vast the resources of his power open to us who trust in him. (Eph. 1.17–19)

These resources are measured by his strength and by the might which he exerted in Christ, where all reality is *made real*. In the light of his being, all goodness is *made good*. We have to pay attention – with our total being open to the being of God. To meditate is to be in a state of empathy with God, in a state of union with him. In God, there is only pure being. As we meditate and sit still, we do not hope, we do not fear, we do not try to love. But our call is to be. We discover that being and loving are one. We realize that God and our spirit are one. We see that there is only the One. Dame Julian in the fourteenth century described prayer as 'the experience of oneing', of being one.

This is why we learn to say our mantra with fidelity and poverty of spirit. It is why we learn to sit so still, so that we can pay attention wholeheartedly, totally, absolutely. Without the attention of an attentive spirit, our religion and any pursuit of a spiritual path remain at the level of theory. To experience it we must learn to attend with the totality of our being. The purity of God is that point where only the clear light of divinity shines. The call to prayer, then, is a call to transcendence. In a sense we can say that within our meditation we transcend ourselves, in the Spirit; we even transcend Christ, in Christ, and enter into the purity of God.

The first important thing to remember is that every one of us is called to this experience. The call of Jesus, indeed the life, death and resurrection of Jesus, are efficacious for all men and women, in all time. All that is required of us is that we attend to the reality of what is achieved by God in Jesus. The power of meditation is its simplicity and its practicality: we take the practical steps to set out on the way leaving the books, the talks, the lectures, the ideas behind and learning to attend in depth. We come to meditation to attend profoundly, learning to be and learning to be in the presence of God, learning from our experience.

What we have seen and heard we declare to you so that you and we together may share in a common life: that life which we share with the Father and his Son, Jesus Christ and we write this in order that the joy of us all may be complete. (1 John 1.3–4)

When we meditate, by our stillness, our discipline and our transcendence, we enter into that sharing in the life of Jesus and his Father.

17

The Secure Base

It is important for all of us to base our life on something really secure. Perhaps everyone is looking for a secure base on which to build his or her life. Probably very early in life we come to know that we cannot find a strong foothold in what is passing away, in what is crumbling.

Some philosophers have expressed this by saying that we can never find our true place in life while we remain prisoners of time and history, because time is passing away and history is passing away. We must pass over and beyond history and learn to transcend time. Not that we reject time or reject history. Indeed, the only way that we can live in time and understand history is if we have a secure base, an unshakable position from which to view time and keep it in perspective. Of course, we must learn to love our world, but we can only love it if we can understand it, seeing it in its true light.

What Christianity proposes to us is this: that the ultimate rock is Christ. He is our secure foothold and united with him we have nothing to fear from history, because we are no longer prisoners of history or time. The Christian vision is not a denial of this life or history, but an openness to the great fact of all history: that time has been intercepted by Christ's love. This is the reality out of which we must live. We can only live from it if we ourselves are open to it in our innermost heart, not through images or concepts, however sacred, but through the reality, the rock that is Christ.

Now this work requires our full attention. It requires all our love. When we meditate we must be as still and as alert as we can be, as open as we can be to the reality in which we have our being. The reality is that the human consciousness of Christ is to be found in our own hearts. We do not have to imagine or confect it. It is the great fact of history: his spirit dwells in our hearts. His human consciousness is our way out of the prison of history and time. It is his consciousness that is our salvation, deliverance and freedom because in our own hearts is to be found the way forward, the way beyond, into infinite expansion of heart and mind. The invitation to this expansion is given to each one of us. If only we take the invitation seriously and act on it by committing ourselves to it. This is why we meditate every morning and every evening: to turn aside from what is passing away and to be more deeply committed to and inserted into what is eternal.

> Their unbelieving minds are so blinded by the god of this passing age, that the gospel of the glory of Christ, who is the very image of God, cannot dawn upon them and bring them light. (2 Cor. 4.4)

It is essential for all of us on the pilgrimage to remember that we cannot vanquish the ego by force. That would itself be egotistical. We cannot use force because force or the pure exercise of willpower would be a self-directed exercise of the will. It would be as though we are trying to possess enlightenment and, therefore, we must understand the dynamic of the egotistical state if we are to escape from its imprisonment.

The principle to bear in mind is this – we cannot possess ourselves but we can *be* ourselves. The ego is self-consciouness and to escape the introverted image of self, to escape from self-obsession, we have to change the direction of our attention, of our consciousness. We have to turn the light around and away from ourselves, beyond ourselves or, perhaps, *through* ourselves. In other words, the only way to transcend the ego is to ignore it.

No amount of self-analysis, self-pity or self-distraction, will overcome the ego. All of these would be much more likely to compound the egotistical state. They are more likely to make us more complex, less free, less capable of being ourselves. The way beyond egoism is the way of total simplicity. Everything that I have said so far is useless as a way of escaping egoism. Why? Because all the things I am saying are just ideas about the ego. But while I am saying them, it is likely that all of us, listening to such ideas, tend to think even more about ourselves. You may agree or disagree with what I have said; but the likelihood, when we listen to such things, is that we think about them and receive them in terms of ourself.

The only way out of the maze is to pass from thought to action. Meditation, the recitation of the mantra as a way of egolessness, is the logical deduction from all we have been saying. In order to stop thinking about ourselves we must enter into the depths of our own being. More than that, we must enter into the depths of being itself. To set out on this journey we have to take our consciousness off ourselves. We have to look beyond ourselves and enter the depths, yes, every morning and every evening.

18

Attention

These words are from the Sermon on the Mount:

> Set your mind on God's kingdom and his justice before everything else, and all the rest will come to you as well. (Matt. 6.33)

'Setting our mind on God's kingdom': two thinkers in recent times, who have had an important influence on our society and who knew what this phrase means, are Simone Weil and E. F. Schumacher. Simone Weil thought that the most important quality we could acquire in our lifetime was what she described as selfless attention. Fritz Schumacher came to the same conclusion and he described the pure attention that Simone Weil speaks about simply as 'attention' – learning to attend. Both of them were influenced by the tradition from which we speak, of meditation: the tradition of contemplative prayer and meditation that comes to us from the early monastic fathers.

The crucial lesson that we have to learn from meditation is to attend wholly and totally, to pay full attention. From reading the Sermon on the Mount we know that each of us must not only change superficially; we must be transformed. We also know from reading St Paul that we can be transformed in Christ, through Christ and with Christ. Now, if you want to change something in your life you have two possibilities open to you. You can try to will that change, and to redirect your life by acts of the will. I think most of us discover from our own experience that our wills are appallingly weak and shockingly inconstant. There is, however, another way.

Everything we see, hear or otherwise experience, is distorted by the prism of our ego. But in learning to say the mantra we learn to leave these limited and distorted perceptions behind. We become absorbed into the divine reality, the oneness which, in his great priestly prayer in the Gospel of John, Jesus speaks of: 'that they may be one as we are one' (John 17.11).

The English medieval mystics spoke of prayer as the process of *oneing*, becoming one by paying undivided attention. Saying the mantra is simply our beginning on the path to this selfless attention. Taking the searchlight of consciousness off ourselves, looking forward, we become like the eye that sees all but cannot see itself. As we begin to see – and here is the extraordinary thing about the Christian vocation – we come to see everything as Christ sees it. In other words, we begin to see it with his light. Listen to his words in the Sermon on the Mount.

> The lamp of the body is the eye. If your eyes are sound you
> will have light for your whole body; if the eyes are bad
> your whole body will be in darkness. (Matt. 6.22–23)

In meditating, we leave behind our own limited view of reality and, by paying full attention to what is, we begin to see everything bathed in that light, the light of truth which is the light of love.

Let me stress for you again the importance of the daily fidelity to meditation every morning and every evening and, at these times, the fidelity to your word. A member of a group of priests with whom I was recently meditating at the monastery, who is just beginning meditation, made a point about this. He said surely if you have a holy thought, a *good* thought while meditating, surely you should follow it. I said the thing to understand is that in saying the mantra with growing and eventually perfect fidelity, we are not attending to *any* thought about God. We are attending to God's real presence in our heart and in all creation. In attending to that presence *any* thought is a distraction. Our invitation is to become wholly absorbed in him, to be one with God.

19

Shiva's Tale of Salvation

I was reading the other day of the Indian God Shiva who was sitting with his wife, looking down on the world, when his wife said to him, 'Why don't you go and grant salvation to some of your devotees?' Shiva said, 'Very well.' And so they went down to a town and sat in the market place. The word got around that a great prophet was there and then the holy people of the town came out.

The first of them came up to Shiva and said, 'I meditate three times every day, in winter I meditate for two hours in cold water, in summer I meditate for two hours in the heat. When will I get salvation?' Shiva looked at him and said, 'Three more incarnations.' You can just imagine the story as this man goes back to his friends, shaking his head and saying, 'Three more, three more.' So it goes on with others. Another person comes and he is told that he has ten more incarnations. Finally a little man comes and he says, 'I am afraid I do not do much but I do try to love everyone around me and I try to love creation. Can I get salvation?' Shiva scratches his head and the little fellow gets a bit nervous and asks again, 'Can I get salvation?' Shiva looks at him and says, 'A thousand incarnations.' At that, the poor fellow jumps for delight and joy and starts shouting to everyone 'I *will* get it, I will get salvation! A thousand, only a thousand more!' At that, he bursts into flames and so does Shiva and his wife and they all become one flame and they are gone.

Then his wife says to him, 'How did that little old man get salvation immediately when you said a thousand incarnations?' He said, 'Yes, that was my ruling; but his generosity overruled my ruling and so he was saved immediately.'

Just after I read this story I picked up the Gospel of Luke and read:

Two men went up to the temple to pray, a Pharisee and the other a tax gatherer. The Pharisee stood up and proclaimed how better he was than other men and the tax collector beside him especially. In his turn, the taxman – a very unpopular job, associated then with exploitation and corruption – simply and humbly acknowledged his need for God's mercy. Jesus said it was he, the sinner, who returned home at rights with God and his own soul. He, in his humility, turned out to be the generous one. (Based on Luke 18.10–14)

We discover – while on the pilgrimage itself – that we are all mere beginners. As St Paul said, we start out in faith, we continue in faith and we arrive in faith. Christian life, the power of the life of Christ within us, is constantly expanding, constantly growing in our hearts. Meditation is an entrance into the nearness of God who is to be found in our hearts. It is also an entrance into God's infinite space. As each of us must discover for ourselves, it is entry into this vast, silent space that is the real power of meditation. From that silence God answers our questions; God answers the yearnings of our heart with the simple answer of love. His love is our hope, our unshakeable confidence, that whatever the difficulty, whatever may be the challenge we face, we can meet it out of the infinite resources he gives us. God does all this within us in silence, if only we will allow the mystery to encompass us.

The quality required for this work is simply *acceptance* of everything that is. 'Whoever seeks his life will lose it and whoever loses it will save it and live' (Matt. 16.25). We must allow these words of Jesus to delve deep into our consciousness. Meditation is just this way of entering into *salvation* and *life*; and we realize it by a commitment to silence.

During Holy Week, each year, as Christians ponder the great mysteries of their faith we all, as modern people, need to face what is perhaps the greatest mystery of all: our own infinite value. The message of this week is to understand our own importance and value and so to understand the importance and value of others. The mystery of our salvation is that God has sent his only Son to save and deliver us from the isolation of our egoism and to deliver us by love into love. We are redeemed by love.

Saying the mantra is a state of humbly accepting that salvation by allowing it to well up within you, laying aside your fears, your questions. Listening only to the heartbeat at the centre of all creation, we find that it is the communication to us of the life of God.

20

Being a Pilgrim

This is from the Gospel of St John:

> If I go and prepare a place for you, I shall come again
> and receive you to myself, so that where I am you may
> be also; and my way there is known to you. Thomas
> said, 'Lord, we do not know where you are going, so
> how can we know the way?' Jesus replied, 'I am the way.'
> (John 14.3–6)

One of our human weaknesses is that we are always trying to settle down. One of the challenges we face in Christian life is to learn to be pilgrims, to be *on the way*. We are
always trying to accumulate things, either material things or
knowledge, but we need to learn instead how to tread the
path of dispossession. It is learning to dispossess ourselves
so that we can continue on the pilgrimage unencumbered.
Jesus described this way of salvation as a narrow road and
'few they are who find it'. The reason why so few do find it
is that it is a comparatively untravelled road. People often ask
me, 'If this way of meditation is so important, why is it that
so few people seem to have heard of it?'

One major commitment is required of the pilgrim. The
pilgrim must not succumb to the temptation to settle down
on the way. 'I have gone far enough. I am getting tired. The
going is getting too tough.' All these feelings, the pilgrim

must set aside. Perhaps the most insidious temptation is for the pilgrim to say, 'This is a good plateau I have arrived at. It's a peaceful place. I'll just rest up here for a bit.' As we continue onwards we learn that our commitment to the pilgrimage *becomes* the pilgrimage. It is never just about 'my perfection' or 'my holiness'. The call that each person has is to become one with the all-whole, all-holy God. The universality of this call and our response to it is the basis of all true community. When we share the silence of our meditation together, each one is transformed. As we travel within and beyond ourselves, each and all of us become one in him. All cultural, social, educational, religious barriers are transcended in the power of love.

There is an old Arabic saying that when a pickpocket sees a saint all he sees is a pocket. In meditation we utterly transcend our cultural conditioning and limitations. We become one in God and we see God in one another because we are willing to learn to see. We are willing to learn to say our mantra and to persevere in the learning. We are willing to learn to be pilgrims and to persevere on the pilgrimage. We are willing to learn to leave self behind. We are willing to learn to be poor in spirit and humble of heart. We are willing to learn to be one.

My children, for a little longer I am with you; then you will look for me and . . . where I am going you cannot come. I give you a new commandment: love one another as I have loved you . . . If there is this love among you, then all will know that you are my disciples. (John 13.33–35)

PART 3

Fully Alive

21

Beginning for the First Time Again

There are two questions that everyone who meditates must face. The first is 'How do you meditate?' The way is absolute simplicity. There is nothing whatever complicated about meditation. Although we may talk a lot about it or use a lot of complicated terms to describe it and its effect, we must always be clear about the absolute simplicity of it. The longer you meditate the more it becomes clear that meditation is simplicity itself.

Let me describe to you again how to meditate. When you meditate take a comfortable posture. Meditation is a discipline and it is a discipline that we in the West are not used to. We are not used to being absolutely still, of sitting still. We are not used to sitting still as a discipline. As a culture we are trained in self-indulgence and we have to learn to be disciplined. The posture, the sitting still, the sitting upright is a first step. Secondly, you must learn to say your word. The word I recommend you to say is 'maranatha' – ma-ra-na-tha. This is an Aramaic word, the language that Jesus spoke and means 'Come, Lord'. In the early Church it was understood to mean 'Come, Lord Jesus'. It is the oldest prayer in the Church and it is the best mantra that I know for any beginner in meditation.

That is enough to know about meditation for the next twenty years. If you can, just stay with that, sit still and say your word, your mantra, from the beginning to the end.

People who have been meditating for a short time, three or four years, often imagine that the time quickly comes when you stop saying your mantra and just rest, staying in silence. What we must learn – and it is best to learn it when you are beginning – is the absolute necessity of saying your word from the beginning to the end. There are all sorts of problems posed for us in that teaching. For example, if you are a Christian, your ego poses the problem for you: 'Is this really prayer? Am I really praying to God now?' If you are not a Christian, your ego poses another question: 'Am I really using this time to the best of my advantage? Shouldn't I be analysing the profound insights that are coming to me?' But what we must learn, whether you are a Christian or not, is that you must be silent. We learn that we have to learn to be silent.

Let us look at the second question: Why should you meditate? Why should anyone meditate? The tradition that brings us together says that, if we are to live life fully, if we are to expand our spirit fully, each of us needs purity of heart. This means that clarity of perception enables us to see reality as it is, to see ourselves as we are, and to see others as they are: the redeemed and loved of God. It means to see God as God is: absolute love. To see all of that we require purity of heart. This involves being able to see straight ahead of us without refracting our vision through the prism of the ego.

Kierkegaard describes purity of heart as the capacity to desire one thing. The one thing we must desire while meditating is to say our mantra, our word. In doing that, we go beyond all the complexities of self-reflective consciousness. This is to be silent and still. For this reason, bodily stillness is so important as a sacrament, an outward sign, of the inward stillness. Purity of heart is simplicity realized. We all need purity of heart if we are to have the humility to see what is before our eyes and to see with absolute clarity of vision.

Let me remind you again: every time we sit down to meditate each of us is a beginner. We begin as if for the first time again. We lay aside all our fears, all anxieties, all hopes, all plans. We lay *everything* aside in order to be open to the supreme purpose of our creation which is to be one, to be one with ourselves, to be one with God and to be one with all creation. The process of meditation is simply that process of becoming one. The way is the way of the one word: ma-ra-na-tha. Do not be discouraged if you find it difficult to stay with the word; but stay with it. Do not be discouraged however many distracting thoughts you find coming into your minds; stay with the word.

To learn to meditate it is necessary to meditate every day, morning and evening. The time I recommend you to meditate for is half an hour twice a day. Do not be discouraged if you fail when you set yourself that routine as a goal but keep returning to it. After thirty years of practice, it is my personal conviction that there is nothing more important for us than to practice this meditation if we are to understand the full wonder of the Christian gospel.

> Therefore, now that we have been justified, through faith, let us continue at peace with God through our Lord Jesus Christ, through whom we have been allowed to enter the sphere of God's grace, where we now stand. (Rom. 5.1–2)

This is what meditation is about: continuing at peace and realizing what has been accomplished through Jesus is that every one of us presently stands in the sphere of God's grace. Meditation is simply the process whereby we try to realize that. We realize it by entering into it, not by thinking about it, not by analysing it, but simply by entering into that sphere of grace by leaving everything else behind. That is the purpose of the word, the mantra: to still our spirit, to still our mind, to be at peace, to be one with God because we stand within God's sphere.

22

Fullness of Life

This is St Paul writing to the Romans:

> May the God of hope fill you with all joy and peace by
> your faith in him, until, by the power of the Holy Spirit,
> you overflow with hope. (Rom. 15.13)

One of the great themes in St Paul's writings is what he calls
the 'fullness of Christ', the *pleroma*. For us this is to experience fullness of life in the power of Jesus which Paul sometimes describes as the 'full measure of the blessing of Jesus'
(Rom. 15.29). What St Paul knows from his experience and
what he encourages us to know from our experience, is that
Christ is the one who contains all blessing within himself.
And he is also the one who communicates the fullness of
blessing to all who 'call upon his name'. The Christian life
can be described as *life in Christ*; and what that means is
that each is invited to live out of his power in union with
him who is the source of all power, all energy. We do so by
being as fully open to his reality as we can be in this life.

The way of meditation is simply the way of being open
to his consciousness. This openness to the consciousness of
Jesus guides each of us to the complete realization of our
potential and our capacity for development in the expansion
of heart and mind. It is even more than that. Through our
union with Christ – this is what St Paul is trying urgently to

communicate to the early Christians – we are connected not just with the source of our own being but of all being and so of all *beings*. The experience of prayer, of being in free-flow connection with the source of our being, rearranges our whole vision of reality. Our vision of the whole of creation is now interpenetrated at every point with the redeeming love of Christ and we are invited to know in our experience in prayer that all are one in the power of that redeeming love.

Our daily meditation is so important because it reveals to each of us individually our inner oneness. By entering into our own spirit we find our oneness with him, with others and with all creation. Putting this another way, we could say that in meditation we advance into the *pleroma*, the full-ness of Christ, and begin to realize that our call is to be one with the cosmic Christ who is all in all. In our prayer and experience of union we do not increase the *pleroma* but we participate in its expansion by expanding ourselves. We are the part of the *pleroma* waiting to be completed and in the power of Christ's love we are expanded into this boundless completion.

What does this mean for you and for me? Why do we say that meditation is this way of expansion into the *pleroma* of Christ? It is the way of expansion because it is the way of selfless attention to the other. It is the way of loss of self because our attention is wholly absorbed in Christ; it is in this absorption that we leave behind all limitation. The New Testament is constantly using extraordinary language, tell-ing us that our mind and his mind are made one. Our heart and his heart are made one. The wonder of this experience is that just as we transcend self by entering into the conscious-ness of Christ, in that very consciousness we transcend even the limitations of Christ's human consciousness. And then, in his glorified consciousness, we go beyond yet again into the mystery that is the Father.

What does fullness need in order to develop? Emptiness. Meditation, as we know from John Cassian, and from the whole of our tradition, is the way of poverty. We have to leave our own 'prayers' behind and enter into *the* prayer of Christ. Our way is the way of the one little word, our mantra. All other words, ideas, thoughts, we surrender and leave behind. Our whole being must enter into this process of emptying. We are emptying out all distractions and all desire so that we may live fully in the mystery of Christ's redemptive love.

When we consider the scheme of and plan of our redemption we can easily be totally intoxicated by the scale on which God has achieved our redemption and our potential for development in the power of Christ. But what we must remember is that it is the daily fidelity to prayer, to our daily meditation, in humility, in poverty and in absolute faithfulness that leads us into the fullness.

May the God of hope fill you with all joy and peace by your faith in him, until, by the power of the Holy Spirit, you overflow with hope. (Rom. 15.13)

Let us be still together in the power of the Holy Spirit.

23

Seeking Truth

This comes from Paul's Second Letter to the Corinthians:

> For the love of Christ leaves us no choice, when once we
> have reached the conclusion that one man died for all and
> therefore all humankind has died. His purpose for dying
> for all was that, while still in this life, we should cease to
> live for ourselves and should live for him who for our sake
> was raised to life. (2 Cor. 5.14–15)

The big problem we all have to face is deciding what is really
important in our lives and what is trivial; to learn to differen-
tiate between what is passing away and what is enduring. The
English medieval writer, John of Salisbury, wrote: 'It is not
possible for one who with their whole heart seeks after truth,
to cultivate what is merely empty.' I think that is the challenge
that each of us has to face – not to cultivate what is empty,
because with our whole heart we seek after truth, after love.

Meditation is important for us today because we live in a
society that is in real danger of losing its sanity. A human
spirit that is healthy demands expansion. All of us need
room to breathe, to expand and to fill our spiritual lungs with
truth and love. If we are healthy, we know that we must cross
all frontiers to what is beyond.

The healthy spirit is the spirit of an explorer. We are not
then terrified by the beyond. We do not feel too tired to seek

what is ahead. The spirit that is really healthy knows that there is no future for us unless we set out whole-heartedly to *explore*.

Meditation is simply a way of coming to that basic healthiness of spirit, in which our spirit has room to breathe, not assailed and weighed down by trivia, or what is merely material. It is a state in which, because we are open to ultimate truth and to ultimate love, we are summoned beyond all mere trivia to live, not out of the shallows but at the source of the river of life where the stream springs up with power and crystal clarity.

The ultimate frontier we are called to cross is the frontier of our own identity; the frontier, in other words, of our own limitations. It is then we are one with all, one with *the* all. To cross this frontier we need to practise, in the depth of our own being, what Jesus teaches: 'The one who would find his life must lose it.' The discipline of the mantra and the discipline of the daily return to prayer is simply that commitment to lose in order to find, to turn aside from everything passing away and to live from the source of all being. This is why we leave behind all images, all thoughts, all ideas and imagination. Why we become as profoundly silent as we can in the presence of the author of life, of love and of sanity.

What each of us must find out, in our own experience, is that the full vision only comes when our heart is set on God. Make no mistake about it, every one of us is summoned to the vision which is the blinding light of God's almighty love. We must learn silence, attention, humility and concentration because the vision is found in our heart. It is not too hard or difficult for us if only we can bring our tiny daily fidelity to the task. This can be the problem with Christians of our day. It seems so much to give a half hour every morning and every evening. It seems too much. But it is nothing compared with the summons to the vision and the love of the one who calls us. If the world is going to be renewed it must be renewed in sanity. If the Church is going to be renewed it must be renewed in sanctity based on sanity. Every one of us is summoned to this basic sanity and to the fullness of sanctity. Never let anyone lead you away from that vision of your life. In prayer we discover our infinite value in God.

> From first to last, this has been the work of God. He has reconciled us to himself through Christ, and he has enlisted us in this service of reconciliation. (2 Cor. 5.18)

We have to learn – and we have to begin again and again – to be humble, to start saying our mantra, to return to it and to continue to return to it.

24

Dispossession

One of the aspects of meditation we have to come to terms with is how to approach it without seeking to gain or to possess anything. We need to try to approach it much more in terms of a total devotion beyond ourselves. Spinoza wrote that 'blessedness is not the reward of virtue. It is virtue itself. We do not find joy in virtue because we control our lusts but, on the contrary, we find joy in virtue because we are able to control our lusts.'

Christians have often approached their spiritual life mainly in terms of reward and possession. Yet the enemy of all spiritual value is desire, seeking reward and seeking to possess. The wisdom that unlocks the spiritual treasure is the spirit of poverty, a spirit of non-possession. Indeed, in meditation we learn to be dispossessed. The spiritual path is one that leads away from self to the other. As we all come to know from our personal experience of meditation, we must tread this path in selfless faith and courage. Learning to say the mantra so that we dispossess ourselves of all thought and all self-consciousness requires devotion. It leads us to absolute liberty because we have left behind all the second-rate values: success, wealth, possession and power.

St John of the Cross expressed it like this: 'When you set your heart on anything, you cease to throw yourself into the All.' In meditation, we are not concerned with the fruit of action but only with humbly saying our mantra. The mantra is thus, the way beyond desire and into union. We do not cease to be human or to be ourselves. Indeed, we become ourselves. The Bhagavad Gita puts it with beautiful humanity:

> Even as all water flows into the ocean but the ocean never overflows, even so the sage feels desires but is ever one with his infinite peace. (2:70)

Because this is what each of us is invited to know, never underestimate your vocation or your capacity. Our capacity is limitless and our vocation is into the mystery of God himself. The infinite peace that we are all called to arises from infinite love. What does this mean?

The openness of God to each one of us is like a vast space into which we expand into his infinity. The call of Jesus is to know this infinite expansion of being. Infinite expansion of being *is* God. All that is required of us is simple fidelity. All that is required of us is that we are serious and that we have our priorities in a sane order: that God is first and last. All that is required of us is that we commit ourselves to his truth and love. Our weakness, like our stupidity, is of no importance because any failing or limitation of ours gives way as we enter into union with him, with his love, with his being. That is what our meditation is: the simple daily return to infinite expansion of spirit in God.

> Your world was a world without hope and without God. But now in union with Christ Jesus you who once were far off have been brought near through the shedding of Christ's blood. For he himself is our peace . . . So he came and proclaimed the good news: peace to you who were far off, and peace to those who were near by; for through him we both alike have access to the Father in the one Spirit. (Eph. 2.12–18)

Bibliography

Useful editions of some books cited are:

Abhishiktananda, *Saccidananda* (a Christian approach to Advaitic Experience), Delhi: ISPCK, 1974.

John Cassian, *Institutes and Conferences*, translated by E. Gibson in 'A Select Library of Nicene and Post-Nicene Fathers of the Christian Church', Second Series, Volume XL, Michigan: Wm B. Eardmans Publishing Co., 1973.

The Cloud of Unknowing, ed. E. Underhill, London: Stuart Wakins, 1970 (original), trans. William Johnston, New York: Image Books, 1973.

New English Bible, Oxford and Cambridge: Oxford University Press with Cambridge University Press, 1970.

Rule of St Benedict, Latin text critical edition, Cuthbert Butler, Freiburg: Herder, 1912, There are many modern translations.

Books and CDs by or about John Main

Books

Christian Meditation: The Gethsemani Talks, John Main, Singapore: Medio Media, 2007.

Community of Love, John Main, Singapore: Medio Media, 2010.

Door to Silence: An Anthology for Christian Meditation, John Main, ed. Laurence Freeman, Norwich: Canterbury Press, 2006.

The Heart of Creation: Meditation: A Way of Setting God Free in the World, John Main, ed. Laurence Freeman, Norwich: Canterbury Press, 2007.

The Hunger for Depth and Meaning: Learning to Meditate with John Main, ed. Peter Ng, Singapore: Medio Media, 2007.

John Main: A Biography in Text and Photos, Paul Harris, Singapore: Medio Media, 2009.

John Main -- By Those Who Knew Him, ed. Paul Harris, Singapore: Medio Media, 2007.

John Main: Essential Writings, ed. Laurence Freeman, New York: Orbis Books, 2002.

John Main: The Expanding Vision, Charles Taylor, Peter Ng, Sarah Bachelard, Yvonne Theroux and others, eds. Laurence Freeman and Stefan Reynolds, Norwich: Canterbury Press, 2009.

The Joy of Being: Daily Readings with John Main, ed. Clare Hallward, USA: Templegate, 1988 (as *John Main: Daily Readings*).

Moment of Christ: Prayer as the Way to God's Fullness, John Main, ed. Laurence Freeman, Norwich: Canterbury Press, 2010.

Monastery without Walls: The Spiritual Letters of John Main, ed. Laurence Freeman, Norwich: Canterbury Press, 2006.

Sacrament – The Christian Mysteries, John Main, Singapore: Medio Media, 2011.

Silence and Stillness in Every Season: Daily Readings with John Main, ed. Paul Harris, Singapore: Medio Media, 2010.

The Way of Unknowing: Expanding the Spiritual Horizons Through Meditation, John Main, Norwich: Canterbury Press, 2011.

Word into Silence: A Manual for Christian Meditation, John Main, ed. Laurence Freeman, Norwich: Canterbury Press, 2006.

Word Made Flesh: Recovering a Sense of the Sacred Through Prayer, John Main, Norwich: Canterbury Press 2009.

CDs

John Main Collected Talks, Singapore: Medio Media, 2012:
 I *Word into Silence*
 II *The Christian Mysteries*
 III *Moment of Christ*
 IV *The Way of Unknowing*
 V *The Heart of Creation*
 VI *Word made Flesh*
 VII *Door to Silence*
 VIII *In the Beginning*
Still Present: The Life and Legacy of John Main, Singapore: Medio Media, 2008.

The Hunger for Depth and Meaning: Learning to Meditate with John Main, compiled by Peter Ng, Singapore: Medio Media, 2007.

The Life and Teachings of John Main, Laurence Freeman, Singapore: Medio Media, 2002.

About the World Community
for Christian Meditation

John Main founded the first Christian Meditation Centre in London in 1975. The World Community for Christian Meditation (WCCM) took form in 1991 after the seed planted then had begun to grow into a far-flung contemplative family. It now continues John Main's vision of restoring the contemplation dimension to the common life of the Church and to engage in dialogue in the common ground shared with the secular world and other religions.

The present director of the Community is Laurence Freeman, a student of John Main and a Benedictine monk of the Olivetan Congregation. The International Centre of the World Community is based in London, with centres in many other parts of the world. The Community is a 'monastery without walls', with both developed national organizations and emerging communities in over a hundred countries. A major building block of all this is the growing number of small, weekly meditation groups which meet in homes, parishes, offices, hospitals, prisons and colleges. They form an ecumenical Christian community of diverse gifts and traditions.

Annually the John Main Seminar and The Way of Peace events bring meditators together in dialogue with other traditions and global movements. The Community also sponsors retreats, schools for the training of teachers of meditation, seminars, lectures and other programmes. It contributes to interfaith dialogue particularly, in recent years with Buddhists and Muslims. A quarterly spiritual letter with news of the Community is mailed and also available online. Weekly readings are available by email, and a growing number of online resources are being developed to help the spiritual journey with the latest technology. This enables new initiatives such as teaching of meditation to children, networking young adult spirituality, and the contemplative dimension of the life of priests. Medio Media is the publishing arm of the community, producing a wide range of books and audio-visual titles to support the practice of meditation.

Meditatio is the outreach of the World Community initiated to mark its twentieth anniversary. Co-ordinated from the Meditatio Centre in London, a programme of seminars will bring a spiritual approach to key social issues of our time such as education, mental health, peace and justice, business, care for those in recovery and the dying. Meditatio is developing the use of technology in the work of spiritual renewal. It will also help with the formation of a younger generation of meditators who will serve later as leaders of the community.

The World Community for Christian Meditation: www.wccm.org

THE WORLD
COMMUNITY FOR
CHRISTIAN MEDITATION
Centres/Contacts Worldwide

For more information about the Community, its work and publications, to join a meditation group, or to learn to meditate, please contact your regional co-ordinator below or the International Centre.

International Centre
The World Community for Christian Meditation
32 Hamilton Road
London W5 2EH
United Kingdom
Tel +44 20 8579 4466
welcome@wccm.org
www.wccm.org

FOR COUNTRIES NOT LISTED BELOW, CONTACT THE INTERNATIONAL CENTRE

Argentina	www.meditacioncristianagrupos.blogspot.com
Australia	www.christianmeditationaustralia.org
Belgium	www.christmed.be
Brazil	www.wccm.com.br
Canada English	www.meditatio.ca
Canada French	www.meditationchretienne.ca
Chile	www.meditacioncristiana.cl
China	www.wccm.hk

Colombia	meditacioncristianacol.blogspot.com
Czech Republic	www.krestanskameditace.cz
Denmark	www.kristenmeditation.org
France	www.meditationchretienne.org
Germany	www.wccm.de
Hong Kong	www.wccm.hk
India	www.wccm-india.org/
Indonesia	www.meditasikristiani.com
Ireland	www.christianmeditation.ie
Italy	www.meditazionecristiana.org
Latvia	www.jesus.lv
Malaysia	www.wccmmalaysia.org
Mexico	www.meditacioncristiana.com
Netherlands	www.wccm.nl
New Zealand	www.christianmeditationnz.org.nz
Norway	www.wccm.no
Poland	www.wccm.pl
Portugal	www.meditacaocrista.com
Singapore	www.wccmsingapore.org
South Africa	www.wccm.co.za
Spain	www.wccm.es
Spain Catalonia	www.meditaciocristiana.cat
Ukraine	www.wccm.org.ua
United Kingdom	www.christianmeditation.org.uk
United States	www.wccm-usa.org
Venezuela	www.meditadores.blogspot.com

Jesus the Teacher Within
Laurence Freeman

978 1 84825 037 6   229 x 152mm   272pp   £14.99

While many people have problems with the church - including most churchgoers - the person of Jesus is an indispensable force in the achievement of any authentic spirituality. The conflict between faith and experience is eased in the rediscovery of the essential unity and simplicity at the heart of Jesus' teachings.

Embarking on this journey of rediscovery, this book takes as its starting point a question that Jesus himself asked his disciples, 'Who do you say I am?' For the many Christians who have never taken this question seriously, Laurence Freeman explores this question in the light of some of the big issues of religious understanding: the historical Jesus, the experiential reading of the Scriptures, personal conversion, and the inner journey.

CANTERBURY
PRESS
Norwich

Available from all good bookshops
or direct from Canterbury Press

Journey to the Heart

Christian Contemplation Through the Centuries - An Illustrated Guide
ed. Kim Nataraja

978 1 84825 108 3   246 x 189mm   448pp   £25.00

The contemplative tradition in Christianity traces its origins back to Jesus himself, who frequently withdrew to quiet places to pray, and it has nourished and challenged disciples in every generation since.

Journey to the Heart is an in-depth and richly illustrated exploration of Christian spirituality by some of today's leading spiritual writers. From New Testament times to the present day, it reveals the life and teachings of the greatest Christian mystics including:

· Jesus, St John and St Paul
· The Early Church Fathers
· Desert Mothers and Fathers
· the early English mystics
· the European tradition
· modern day rediscoverers

Available from all good bookshops
or direct from Canterbury Press